OUR ENGLISH BIBLE IN THE MAKING

 OUR

ENGLISH BIBLE

in the MAKING

the word of life in living language

 herbert Gordon may

Published for the
Cooperative Publishing Association
by
THE WESTMINSTER PRESS, PHILADELPHIA

This is one of a series of books produced for interdenominational use by the Protestant denominations working through the Cooperative Publishing Association.

PREFACE

There are many books on the history of the English Bible. But there is need for a short book on this subject that is not too detailed or too technical and yet presents enough of the information concerning Biblical manuscripts and translations to give the general reader adequate perspective and some basis for personal judgment on English translations of the Bible. This is one of the reasons for the publication of this book.

Yet it is not the chief reason. This book is written in the hope that the story of the making of the English Bible as presented here will assist the reader to a better understanding of the nature of the Bible. The ultimate aim of the book is a more adequate appreciation of the Word of God. It is hoped that the facts and personalities presented here may not only suggest to the reader something of the influence of the Bible through the centuries, but may also act as an inspiration for spiritual growth. For this reason the book may not improperly be designated a handbook for Christian education. May those who read this little volume come to a better understanding of the significance of the Bible for the Christian faith and find encouragement to make use of the Bible.

This book appears at an important point in the history of the translation of the Bible into English. This year, 1952, is the year of the publication of the complete Revised Standard Version. Although two chapters of the book are devoted to it, our primary intent has not been to describe and evaluate this new translation. The chief motivation of the book remains that indicated in the second paragraph of this Preface.

At various points the author has expressed his indebtedness to the excellent work of John Eadie, *The English Bible* (London: The

Macmillan Company, 1876, 2 vols.). Besides original sources, such recent books as the following have been consulted, and the general reader who is interested in further study will find them useful: Ira M. Price, *The Ancestry of Our English Bible,* Second Revised Edition, by W. A. Irwin and Allen P. Wikgren (Harper & Brothers, 1949); Sir Frederick Kenyon, *Our Bible and the Ancient Manuscripts* (Harper & Brothers, 1940); H. W. Robinson, Editor, *The Bible in Its Ancient and English Versions* (Clarendon Press, 1940); C. C. Butterworth, *The Literary Lineage of the King James Bible* (University of Pennsylvania Press, 1941); Stanley Rypins, *The Book of Thirty Centuries* (The Macmillan Company, 1951). Special attention should be called to Luther A. Weigle's *The English New Testament from Tyndale to the Revised Standard Version* (Abingdon-Cokesbury Press, 1949). For an important collection of source materials from 1525 to 1611, see A. W. Pollard, *Records of the English Bible* (Oxford University Press, 1911).

The author would express gratitude to a number of persons who have read this manuscript, including Dean Emeritus Luther A. Weigle, of Yale University Divinity School; Professor Harold R. Willoughby, of the Divinity School of the University of Chicago; Professor Frederick B. Artz, of Oberlin College; and Dr. John Middaugh, of Cleveland.

HERBERT GORDON MAY.

CONTENTS

OUR ENGLISH BIBLE IN THE MAKING

I ✍

THE BIBLE IN THE MOTHER TONGUE

THE NEED FOR TRANSLATION

THIS is your story. The Christian Church is a fellowship of believers, a community of the faithful. The special revelation of God to mankind in history, culminating in the life and teachings of Jesus and the appearance of that community of the faithful (*communio sanctorum*) is recorded in the Book. Through that Book, God is speaking to the Christian community today. Christianity is a religion of the Book. The Scriptures belong to " the people of the Lord."

It is incredible that it could ever have been thought otherwise than this; yet there have been those who would have withheld the Scriptures from the people, believing that church members could not be trusted to interpret them for themselves, or thinking that the authority of the priestly dignitaries or the dogma of the Church overshadowed in importance the Scriptures themselves. It was even believed that to translate the Bible into a language that the people could understand or to read the Bible in English was heresy. We today would take for granted Wycliffe's view that the Scriptures should be " the property of the people, and one which no party should be allowed to wrest from them." We find it difficult to understand how a learned man might say to Tyndale that it is better to be without God's law than the pope's, or how a bishop might thank God that he never knew what the Old or the New Testament was. Parliament passed restrictive acts against translating and reading the Bible, and many suffered the torments of torture and of burning at the stake for possessing and reading a copy of the Scriptures.

The story of the translation of the Bible into English is an important part of the struggle of democracy against autocracy and liberty against dictatorship, both in the field of politics and in the field of religion. The right of the people to have and to read the Bible in their own language involved the issue of freedom of speech and freedom of religion. It concerned the freedom of the individual conscience and the theological question whether faith alone justifies before God. We shall find that at times the Bible in the vernacular, or common tongue, was circulated against the will of the authorities, both ecclesiastical and State, while the common people received it gladly, discussing it avidly wherever people gathered, on the streets and in the alehouses and taverns.

The early translators realized the wider issues that were at stake in this matter of putting the Bible into the language of laymen. At that time the message of the Bible was locked up in the ecclesiastical tongue, Latin, the language of the official translation, and not even all the clergy could read Latin with ease. Wycliffe believed that possession and study of the Bible by the layman was the truest safeguard and charter of national and ecclesiastical independence, and was not unrelated to the problems of the oppression of the industrial classes into pauperism. Tyndale wrote that he had " seen by experience how it was impossible to establish the lay people in any truth, except the Scripture were plainly laid before their eyes in their mother tongue." But those who had little confidence in or regard for the common man, and who had an exaggerated view of their own prerogatives and superiorities and of the wisdom of the privileged educated few, deplored the fact that " the gospel pearl is cast abroad and trodden under the foot of swine," in the words of one of Wycliffe's contemporaries.

Many people today who are secularly minded and Biblically quite illiterate, though they may be well informed on other subjects, little realize the role that the Bible has played in the history of the development of the freedoms which they cherish, both through the inspiration of its content and through the struggle to make it available to mankind. For this reason this is the story of everyman. It is not just a tale about scholars, translators, Church dignitaries, kings, manuscripts, and languages. It is about the merchants, tailors, bakers, and " uther tempral men " who considered themselves " sufficient doctor of themselfs to reid and understand the hie mysteries of the Bible," and women who could not sew, card, or spin without learning the same from other skillful women but dared to " usurp to reid and interpret the Bible," and who are deplored in words such as these by a Scottish priest in 1601.

The Bible was written to be read by such as these, not merely by clerics and Biblical scholars. The Bible was originally written in the language of the people. The Old Testament was written for the Hebrews in the Hebrew language. A small portion of it was written in the related Semitic language, Aramaic, for we find that, in the Hebrew Old Testament, Ezra 4:8 to 6:18; 7:12–26; Dan. 2:4b to 7:28; Jer. 10:11 are not in Hebrew, but in Aramaic, written at the time when Aramaic had become the vernacular tongue of the Jews, as it was also at the time of Jesus in Palestine. And since the Early Church flourished in Greek-speaking communities, the Epistles were written in Greek, and the stories of Jesus and of the spread of Christianity in the Gospels and The Acts were also written in Greek. The Bible was to become the Scriptures of people speaking many different tongues, and so translations became necessary. Although we are here primarily interested in the translation of the Scriptures into our own tongue, we must have as background an outline of the story of the more important earlier translations of the Bible into the vernacular tongue.

The Bible in Greek

The Jews, like the Christians, are " a people of the Book." When Hebrew was in the process of becoming a literary rather than a living language, and many of the Jews were speaking Greek as their everyday tongue, it was natural that a Greek translation should be made. A letter of a certain Aristeas, who lived about 100 B.C., tells a story of how the Pentateuch (i.e., the Torah or Law, the books from Genesis to Deuteronomy) was translated by seventy-two elders, six from each of the twelve tribes of Israel, who were brought from Palestine to Alexandria in Egypt, because Ptolemy II, king of Egypt from 285 to 246 B.C., wanted a copy of the Pentateuch in Greek for his famous library in Alexandria. These seventy-two men took seventy-two days to complete their work. At a celebration of its completion, in recognition of the sacredness and accuracy of the translation, a curse was pronounced on anyone who should make any alterations in it.

This story may be almost entirely legendary, and was perhaps told to give authority to a revised standard Greek translation which was made about 100 B.C. It may, however, reflect the actual making of a complete translation of the Pentateuch about 250 B.C. for the Jewish community by Alexandrian Jews. It has been surmised that there may have been a number of early Greek translations. A later legend told how the seventy-two translators were shut up each in a separate cell or two in a cell, and each worked separately on the translation of the Old Testament into Greek. When they came forth, they found that, lo and behold, their translations agreed word for word! Such a story was told to give authority to the translation. Whenever a translation is made, the question of its authority as over against the authority of the original or of earlier translations naturally arises.

It is clear that at first the Pentateuch was translated into Greek, and then gradually the other books; by 132 B.C. most of the Old Testament existed in Greek translation, as is suggested by the Prologue to Ecclesiasticus, one of the books of the Apocrypha. Because of the association of the number seventy (seventy-two) with it, the early Greek translation is known as the Septuagint, or Version of the Seventy. It was to become the Bible of the Early Christian Church. Other Greek translations were made, such as those of Aquila, Theodotion, and Symmachus in the second and third centuries A.D., to which, along with the Septuagint, one may find reference in the margin of the Revised Standard Version. These early versions are important in the study of the Biblical text.

THE BIBLE IN ARAMAIC

The Aramaic versions are known as Targums, i.e., "Translations." They were made to meet the needs of the Aramaic-speaking Jews. Aramaic had become the common tongue of many of the Jews. From as early as the fifth century B.C. there are preserved the records of a Jewish colony in Egypt at Syene at the First Cataract on the Nile, and these business, legal, and literary documents are in Aramaic. The Aramaic Targums are an expression of the desire to have the Scriptures in the vernacular, the familiar spoken tongue, that they might be understood by the people. Their origin may go back as far as the time of Ezra, for the explanations made at the occasion of the reading of the law (Neh. 8:8) may have been in Aramaic. The Targums are often not strictly translations, but may be free and expansive interpretations, as when in the Palestinian Targum a single verse may be elaborated to fill a half page of the manuscript.

There are in existence Targums to all the books except Daniel, Ezra, and Nehemiah. There are, for instance, the Targum Onkelos to the Pentateuch and the Targum Jonathan to the Prophets, which represent official texts established in the fifth century A.D. There is also a Jerusalem Targum to the Pentateuch, of which fragments were found in recent times in Cairo, Egypt. "Onkelos" is Aquila and "Jonathan" is a translation of the Greek name Theodotion, but the authorship indicated by these titles is probably fictitious. It is presumed that the text of these two official Targums was more probably fixed by commissions. There are probable indications that Aramaic Targums of the Pentateuch and the Prophets existed in written form in pre-Christian times.

THE BIBLE IN SYRIAC

A most important early translation of the Bible into the vernacular is the Syriac Bible, which is still in use in some branches of the Eastern Churches. The standard Syriac translation is called the Peshitta, meaning "simple," or "common." The translation of the Syriac Old Testament has been associated with the city of Edessa in northern Mesopotamia, but perhaps it should be connected with the region of Adiabene, east of the Tigris, where in the first century A.D. there was a famous queen named Helena, who became a convert to Judaism. It may be that the Syriac Old Testament is of Jewish origin, although scholars are in disagreement at this point. The date of its origin is also obscure, but parts of a Syriac Old Testament may be as early as the middle of the first century A.D. It became the Scripture of the Syrian Christians before the third century. It was subject to later revisions. There were other Syriac translations, including one made from the Septuagint. The Peshitta

Old Testament is particularly important because it is a translation from one Semitic language, Hebrew, into another Semitic language, Syriac. This makes possible a more exact reproduction of words and idioms than in the Septuagint, which is a translation from a Semitic to an Indo-European tongue.

The New Testament, originally written in Greek, was also translated into Syriac, that the Syriac-speaking Christians might have the Bible in the vernacular. There is a Syriac harmony of the Gospels dated to the second century, an Old Syriac version of the Gospels not later than the second century, and the complete revision of the New Testament in Syriac to produce an authorized standard text by Rabbula, bishop of Edessa, at the beginning of the fifth century. This last is called the Peshitta New Testament. Syriac is a dialect of Aramaic, and may be called Eastern Aramaic. It is thus very similar to the language spoken by Jesus and his contemporaries in first century Palestine.

THE BIBLE IN LATIN

For over a century the Christian community at Rome used Greek, Paul had written his Epistle to the Romans in Greek, and many of the early Christians in Rome were Greek in origin. It was not until the end of the second century that theological discussions were written in Latin, although Latin was to become the official language of the Church, as it still is in the Roman Catholic Church today. The first Latin translation of the Bible, called the Old Latin Version, arose probably in northern Africa, made for the Latin-speaking Christians there. It is known to have existed by the middle of the third century, although parts of the Bible may have been translated earlier. The Old Testament of the Old Latin Version was a translation, not from the Hebrew, but from the Greek Septuagint, although it is probable that Jewish-Christian converts who knew Hebrew may have had some hand in it.

But the Latin translation that was to remain the official version of the Church up to modern times was the Vulgate. It was the work of Jerome, who lived A.D. 346–420. He was commissioned by Pope Damascus to revise the Old Latin Version. He completed the Gospels in 383, and the New Testament was finished in 391. It was a revision of the Old Latin Version by comparing it with the Greek. He also revised the Old Latin Psalter. After Pope Damascus died, Jerome went to Palestine where he lived in Bethlehem. Here he made another revision of the Psalter, as well as other books of the Old Testament. But in the course of his work Jerome came to realize that a translation of a translation was not enough, and that an adequate translation of the Old Testament must be based on the original Hebrew. He had the advantage of studying Hebrew under a Jewish rabbi, and he was well equipped to make the translation. Although he was interrupted by severe illness, he completed the translation in the year 405. Besides the canonical books (i.e., those in our Protestant Bibles today and recognized as Scripture), he translated the books of Tobit and Judith, which belong to the Apocrypha or noncanonical books.

At first his translation was met with antagonism, and it was even declared to be heretical. The renowned Church theologian Augustine at first had his doubts about it. Its reception has parallels in the history of the Bible, when efforts to make a better translation have met with enmity and misunderstanding, and the older translation has been looked upon as more authoritative because it was older and had come to be the tradition. But Jerome's translation, after his death, became the Bible of the Roman Church, and we shall have many occasions to refer to it later. Jerome had not included the books of the Apocrypha in his Bible, but the Roman Church added the Old Latin Version of the Apocryphal books to make its complete Bible. The New Testament used was Jerome's revision of the Old Latin. This official translation of the Latin Bible is called the Vulgate, from the Latin word *vulgatus,* meaning " common."

All these ancient versions which we have been describing are significant not only as illustrations of the need for adequate translations in the mother tongue, but they are also important for the Biblical scholar who is interested in trying to recover the readings in the ancient Hebrew manuscripts which these translations reflect. And the reader of the Revised Standard Version of the Old Testament will find of interest the marginal references to these translations, as they have been used by the translators.

There were other early translations of the Bible into the vernacular, such as the translations into Coptic, Ethiopic, Armenian, Gothic, Slavic, and Arabic, but we must now turn to our main subject and begin by considering the earliest efforts to provide a translation of the Scriptures into the vernacular in England.

EARLY TRANSLATIONS IN ENGLAND

This is a story of small but important beginnings. It starts in the eighth to tenth centuries with the Anglo-Saxon versions, and it is concerned with such men as Caedmon, Aldhelm, Bede, King Alfred, and others. Augustine, who became archbishop of Canterbury, had arrived in England in A.D. 597. He had been sent as missionary by his friend Pope Gregory the Great.[1] The consequent revival of Christianity there, stimulated by missionaries from Rome and Ireland, aroused a desire to know the Word of God. Most of the people could not read, and there was no immediate call for a translation of the Bible in English.

An illiterate peasant, Caedmon, near the end of the seventh century was in the abbey at Whitby. Feeling himself unable to take his turn with his companions in the singing at the table, he had gone out to the stables to care for the beasts. He heard a voice saying, " Caedmon, sing something to me! " Asking what he should sing, he was told, " Sing of the beginning of created things." Inspired by this vision, Caedmon turned into verse the history of Genesis, the Exodus from Egypt, the entrance into the Promised Land, and other narratives which he had learned from those who taught the Scripture, including of course the story of Jesus and the apostles. He sang his alliterative lines of verse to the accompaniment of his harp, with the endeavor to pull men from their love of wickedness and to stir them with the love and readiness to do well. Such is the story told by Bede (see below).

[1] The story should be told of how Gregory had seen for the first time three fair and handsome youths with " noble heads of hair " put up for sale in Rome. On inquiry he found that they were from the island of Britain. Gregory bemoaned that such lightsome countenances were subject to the author of darkness (i.e., that they were pagans). He asked how their nation was called. When told they were called " Angles," he said, " They are well called, for they have the face of angels, and are worthy to be fellow-heirs with the angels in heaven."

Aldhelm was the abbot of Malmesbury and later bishop of Sherborne, and he was a gifted musician. It is said that when the peasantry did not care for his sermons, he attracted his audience by standing in the garb of a minstrel upon a bridge over which the people had to pass, singing to them what they would not listen to in sermon form. He made a translation of The Psalms into Anglo-Saxon about A.D. 700, and so may be said to be the first to translate the Bible into the vernacular in England.

Bede, whom a modern scholar calls the most shining light of learning in western Europe during the eighth century, translated the Gospel of John into Anglo-Saxon. It is uncertain whether he translated from the Latin Vulgate or the original Greek, for no part of his translation exists today. A touching story is told of how he finished the translation on his bed on the day of his death on Ascension Day in 735. Finally, one sentence remained to be done, and when it was finished, at his request, Bede was laid on the pavement of his cell opposite the place where he was in the habit of praying, and breathed his last with the " Gloria " on his lips.

King Alfred was not only a great king, but he was also a scholar, and he should be placed among these early translators. He prefixed to his code of laws a translation (from the Latin) of the Ten Commandments and portions of the succeeding chapters of Exodus and a short passage from The Acts It is said that at the time of his death in 901 he was working on a translation of The Psalms.

It is not surprising that special attention was given to The Psalms and the Gospels by translators in this early period. Around A.D. 700 Bishop Egbert made a translation of the Gospels. There are interlinear (i.e., between the lines) translations of the Gospels, such as the Anglo-Saxon paraphrase made by the priest Aldred about 950 between the lines of an earlier text in Old Latin. From about the same time there is a translation of the Gospels apart from the Latin text on which it was based. Around the year 1000, Aelfric, archbishop of Canterbury, translated portions of the Old Testament, including the books from Genesis to Joshua, omitting sections of lesser interest, and in a series of sermons or homilies gave renderings from other books, Judges, Kings, Job, Esther, and the Maccabees.

This is not the complete story of the translations into Anglo-

Saxon, and we shall not dwell here upon the translations into Early English after the Norman conquest, such as a metrical version of the Gospels and The Acts in the thirteenth century and translations of the Psalter in the first half of the fourteenth century. But the stage is now set for the appearance of the first English translation of the entire Bible. It is to a large extent the story of John Wycliffe.

The First Complete Bible in English

John Wycliffe was born in Hipswell in Yorkshire, perhaps sometime after the generally accepted date, 1324. He enrolled at Balliol College at Oxford, and became master of Balliol, achieving recognition as the most able theologian on the faculty. In 1374 he was appointed by the king to the rectory at Lutterworth. He opposed the interference of the Church dignitaries, particularly the pope, in politics, and protested against the wealth of the Church and of its high dignitaries. Arousing their antagonism, he was summoned to appear before the bishop of London. In one year Pope Gregory XI issued five bulls ordering that Wycliffe be arrested and examined. When the chancellor at Oxford was ordered by Gregory to arrest Wycliffe and his followers, the university only appeared to give consent, the vice-chancellor asking Wycliffe not to go out because he wished no one else to arrest him, and Wycliffe agreed.

Wycliffe was a reformer, firmly opposed to the usurpation or seizing of powers by Rome. He emphasized that the Church was the whole company of the elect, with Christ alone as its head. He wrote prolifically in Latin and in English. The trend of his writings is suggested in his work, *The Thirty-three Conclusions on the Poverty of Christ,* in which he protested against priests' accepting secular employment, objected to civil rule by the papal office, and maintained that rulers could take property from the pope or the cardinals when they abused their privileges.

He believed that the Scriptures were a sufficient rule of life apart from canon law, and that every man, whether clergyman or layman, had the right to examine the Bible for himself. No man, he said, was " so rude a scholar but that he might learn the words of the gospel according to his simplicity." He would have the Bible accessible to every man in his own tongue, for he believed the Scriptures to be "the property of the people."

He established an order of Poor Priests or itinerant or wandering preachers to go forth barefoot, in undressed wool, without purse and with a long staff in their hands, to carry his message to the people. One antagonist called them "wolves in sheep's clothing." Among these poor priests was a certain Swinderby, whose pulpit at one time was between two millstones. The followers of Wycliffe were called Lollards. The meaning of the word "Lollard" has been variously interpreted, and it may most probably mean one who chants or says prayers, but it was purposely confused with a Middle English word meaning "a loafer," and with the Latin *lolia,* "tares."

Just how much of the actual translation of the Wycliffe Bible was made by Wycliffe himself is uncertain, although the inspiration for it certainly came from him, and his contemporaries looked upon it as his Bible. The New Testament was completed first, appearing around the year 1382, and the complete Bible was issued two years later, around 1384. This event marks the birth of the first complete English Bible. The Wycliffe Bible included the Apocryphal books, and was a translation, not from the original languages, but from the Vulgate, the official Latin version. It was certainly not all translated by Wycliffe, for he enlisted the help of other scholars. Nicholas of Hereford did the Old Testament from Genesis to Baruch 3:20, stopping there probably because at that point he was summoned to answer a charge of heresy. Some believe that Wycliffe was the translator of the New Testament and of the rest of the Old Testament after Baruch 3:20. This latter is particularly uncertain, in view of the state of Wycliffe's health at the time.

In his last years, Wycliffe suffered terribly from rheumatism, and he was partially paralyzed due to a stroke. Despite his physical condition, conscious of the attacks on his Poor Priests and the antagonisms toward him, his pen was very active. He had another stroke and was paralyzed when he was listening to Mass in his church at Lutterworth on December 29, 1384, and he died on the last day of that year.

Following the death of Wycliffe, a revision of the translation was made. The earliest existing manuscript of the whole work belongs to 1408, although parts of it certainly appeared earlier. The reviser was probably John Purvey, who had been Wycliffe's secretary at Lutterworth. Purvey was also a "reformer," and was honored by having writs issued to seize his writings and those of Hereford and of another associate, Ashton. There are today in existence around 170 copies of the Wycliffe Bible, most of them being Purvey's revision. They are all in manuscripts written by hand, for the printing press had not yet been invented. Judging by the costly appearance of many of these manuscripts, they were often bought by the wealthier people. Wycliffe's Bible remained the popular Bible, despite the strong opposition to it, until Tyndale's translation appeared in the sixteenth century.

And there was opposition. Knighton, canon of Leicester, protested that "this Master Wycliffe translated from Latin into English — the Angle and not the angel speech — the Scriptures which Christ gave to the clergy and doctors of the Church that they might sweetly minister to the laity and to weaker persons." Archbishop Arundel of Canterbury, who forbade on penalty of prison anyone in his jurisdiction to read Wycliffe's works, and under whose inspiration a Convocation Constitution decreed that "no man shall, hereafter, by his own authority, translate any text of the Scripture into English," described Wycliffe as "that wretched and pestilent fellow, the son of a serpent, the herald and child of Antichrist, John Wycliffe."

The Council of Constance in 1415, which condemned John Hus to the stake, condemned the writings of Wycliffe to be burned and ordered his bones to be dug out of the consecrated ground. And so it happened that, in 1428, Wycliffe's bones were disinterred and burned to ashes, and cast into the river Swift. But as that stream continued to flow, so Wycliffe's work and influence continued to be felt. A man of unimpeachable character, of undaunted personal courage, who was in the best sense a reformer, Wycliffe was a person worthy to inspire the first English translation of the complete Bible.

II ✍

THE BEGINNINGS OF THE PRINTED ENGLISH BIBLE

WYCLIFFE AND TYNDALE

THE father of the later authorized versions of the Bible was not
John Wycliffe, despite his great importance in the history of
the English Bible, but rather William Tyndale. The Wycliffe Bible
was a translation of a translation, while the translations "in the
tradition" are largely from the original Hebrew and Greek. The
English of the time of Wycliffe seems very strange to a modern
reader. This can be appreciated by those who have read Chaucer's
Canterbury Tales, written in the same fourteenth century. Many
Latinized terms in the Wycliffe Bible make that translation still
more foreign to us, for we find there such words as spelong (cave),
sellis (chairs), sudarie (napkin), and gemels (twins). Yet a change
of spelling will give many of the words in the Wycliffe Bible a more
familiar aspect, as in the case of boyschel (bushel), carkeis (carcass),
or yuel (evil).

We may indicate something of the difference between the Wycliffe
Bible and the translation by Tyndale by comparing Matt. 5:3,5 in
the two versions. The Wycliffe Bible reads:

"Blessid *be* the pore in spirit, for the kingdam in heuenes is heren."

"Blessid *be* mylde men, for thei shuln welde the eerthe." The
Tyndale New Testament reads:

"Blessed are the poore in sprete, for theirs is the kyngdome off
heven.

"Blessed are the meke, for they shall inheret the erth." It is indicative of the influence of Tyndale's translation that his rendering
of these verses, apart from the spelling, is identical with that of the
Revised Standard Version.

Tyndale's Contemporaries

William Tyndale belongs to the age of the Renaissance and the Protestant Reformation. The Renaissance had resulted in new interest in classical learning. Between the time of Wycliffe and that of Tyndale printing had been invented. The time of Tyndale was also that of Erasmus, Luther, and Sir Thomas More, the time of Thomas Cromwell, Archbishop Cranmer, and Henry VIII. It was a day of New Learning, and to some it seemed like the advent of the golden age. Gutenberg had earlier set up the first printing press to use movable type, and around 1452-1456 he had issued from it the first book printed in Europe. This was the Gutenberg Bible, usually called the Mazarin Bible because a copy of it was found in the library of Cardinal Mazarin. This Bible was a copy of the Latin Vulgate.

The fact that now Bibles could be reproduced with less difficulty and more cheaply was to mean much for the circulation of the sacred Scriptures among the people, and an important instrument was provided for those interested in the Bible in the vernacular. The first part of Luther's famous translation of the Bible into German was published in 1522. The great scholar of the day was Erasmus, who had come to Cambridge in 1511 to teach Greek. He edited the corrected Greek text of the New Testament that Tyndale was to use. It was published in 1516, accompanied by a Latin translation.

Tyndale in England

Tyndale was born around 1494 in Gloucestershire. He studied at first at Oxford, and then moved to Cambridge, attracted there by the fame of Erasmus. When he left Cambridge, he became a schoolmaster to the children of the knight of Gloucestershire, Sir John Walsh. It was a rural house, and the oldest of the children was six years of age. At the table of Sir John Walsh, Tyndale came into contact with many Church leaders, with whom he loved to argue theology and by whom he came to be considered heretical. He protested against ignorant priests who knew no more of Latin " than they read in their portesses and missals." He became convinced of the need of a translation into English from the original tongues, and he swore to a " learned man " that if God spared his life he would make the boy who drove the plow know more about the Scriptures than did the learned man himself. Erasmus, disagreeing with those who were unwilling that the Bible be translated into the vulgar (i.e., common) tongue and read by private persons, had in similar vein wished " that the plowman would sing a text of Scripture at his plowshare, and the weaver at his loom with this would drive away the tediousness of time."

Leaving the Walsh home, Tyndale went to London and hoped to enter the service of Tunstall, bishop of London. But the bishop refused his request, and Tyndale was befriended by a London merchant, Humphrey Monmouth, who had heard Tyndale preach in London in the Church of St. Dunstan-in-the-West, and who took Tyndale into his house. Four and one half years later Monmouth was to be arrested and thrown into the London Tower, charged with heresy and accused of having given succor to Tyndale. Monmouth, in his request for release, described Tyndale as " a good priest. . . . He studied most part of the day and of the night at his book, and he would eat but sodden meat by his good will, and drink but single small beer." Monmouth paid Tyndale ten pounds to pray for his father and his mother.

FIRST PRINTED ENGLISH NEW TESTAMENT AND ITS RECEPTION

Tyndale stayed in London a year. He states that he saw that there was no place in " my lord of London's palace " to do the work of translating the New Testament, and that there was not even any place in all of England to do it. So he left England and went to Hamburg in Germany, to set about the work of translation. From Hamburg he went to Wittenberg, where Luther was, and remained there for almost a year. After returning to Hamburg, he went to Cologne in 1525, and there he found a printer for his New Testament, a man named Peter Quentel. But an enemy of the Reformation, Johann Dobnek or Cochlaeus, by the ruse of plying some of the printers with wine at his dwelling, learned that there were on press three thousand copies of " the Lutheran New Testament " through the generosity of English merchants who had plans to convey the volumes secretly to England. He obtained an injunction against proceeding with the work, and Tyndale and his assistant,

Friar William Roye, fled to the city of Worms with the incomplete printed sheets. There printing was resumed and completed, probably beginning anew a completely fresh edition.

Thus in 1525 or 1526 appeared the first printed English New Testament. The copies were transported in secret to England, placed in cases of merchandise. The small (octavo) volume of Tyndale's New Testament could be purchased at a reasonable cost, and the common people received it gladly. But it was bitterly attacked by the ecclesiastical authorities. Tunstall, bishop of London, said he could find 2,000 errors in it, and issued an injunction stating that certain children of iniquity belonging to Luther's sect had "with crafty trickery" translated into English the holy gospel of God, and he ordered that all copies be collected and burned. A cardinal from Rome wrote that no holocaust, no burnt offering, could be more pleasing to God. The English ambassador was instructed by Cardinal Wolsey to burn all the copies he could and to have the printer at Antwerp banished and his property confiscated. But the lords of Antwerp released the imprisoned printer, whose name was Endhoven, and would not burn the books. During Endhoven's imprisonment an issue of the New Testament by another printer was smuggled off in grain ships.

A London merchant and friend of Tyndale in Antwerp, named Augustine Packington, agreed to buy up for Bishop Tunstall copies of the New Testament at the bishop's expense that they might be burned. But at the same time he was conspiring with Tyndale, who agreed to provide him with the copies of the New Testament, for, said Tyndale: "These two benefits will come thereof: I shall get money of him for these books, to bring myself out of debt, and the whole world will cry out upon the burning of God's Words — and the overplus of the money that shall remain to me, shall make me more studious to correct the said New Testament, and so newly to imprint the same once again, and I trust the second will much better like [please] you than ever did the first." If the story is true, the bishop, as the chronicler says, thought he had God by the toe, when he had the devil by the fist. Of course the burning of the New Testaments only increased interest in them.

Sir Thomas More entered into literary debate against Tyndale, and accused him of corrupting and changing the New Testament from the doctrine of Christ to "deuylysh heresyes," and said it was really not the New Testament but "Tyndals testament or Luthers testament," charging that it was made "after Luthers counsayle." One cannot doubt the sincerity of More, and More himself was to die a martyr to his faith. He was imprisoned in the Tower of London and beheaded because he refused to compromise his Roman Catholic principles. He would not take an oath to support the Act of Succession, which he felt meant a repudiation of the proper authority of the pope and a denial of the validity of the king's marriage to Catherine. His courage in prison at his execution matches that of Tyndale. In the debate between the two, Tyndale's arguments move on a higher level in general than More's, although at times the debate degenerated into mutual revilings. More believed it right for Tyndale's books and "the likers of them" to be burned, and called Thomas Hitton, who had been burned at the stake, "the devil's stinking martyr."

TYNDALE'S OTHER WORKS

Tyndale's plans included a translation of the Old Testament from the original Hebrew, and he published in 1530 the translation of the Pentateuch (Genesis to Deuteronomy), and in the following year The Book of Jonah was issued. He not only added to a revision of the New Testament in 1534 a translation of Old Testament passages read as epistles in the Church liturgy, and also revised his translation of the Pentateuch, but he most probably worked on the translation of the books from Joshua to Second Chronicles. The 1534 revision of the New Testament is described by Westcott as "altogether Tyndale's noblest monument." In the preface, "W. T. vnto the Reader," Tyndale stated that he revised it "with all dylygence, and compared it vnto the Greke, and have weded oute of it many fautes, which lacke of helpe at the begynninge and oversyght, dyd sowe therin." Characteristically, he says that if he learned of himself or from others of anything that escaped him or might be more plainly translated, he would "shortlye after cause it to be mended." Another revision was made by him in 1535, and the care he showed in such work illustrates the quality of his scholarship.

The translation of Joshua to Chronicles was not published until after his death.

Tyndale published other things besides his translations, and when he was martyred, the basis of the accusation was not his translations but what were regarded as his heresies. He published the *Parable of the Wicked Mammon* in 1528, *Obedience of a Christen Man* in 1528, and *Practyse of Prelates* in 1530, besides his *Answer to More* in 1531 and expositions of I John and of Matthew, and also smaller works. *Practyse of Prelates* was directed against the divorce of Catherine by King Henry, and was also an indictment of the clergy. Improvement in the attitudes toward the Bible in English before his death is indicated in the fact that with the consent of Thomas Cromwell and with a dedication to the king, Coverdale's Bible (see p. 33) was published in 1535.

In 1531, Tyndale informed the king through Stephen Vaughan, whom the king had asked to persuade Tyndale to retract and come back to England, that if the king would grant that " only a bare text of the Scriptures " be put forth among the people, by any translator that the king pleased, he, Tyndale, would promise to write no more and would return to England to offer his body to suffer pain and torture or whatever death the king willed. Better than anything else, this shows how the consuming passion of Tyndale was for the circulation of the Bible in English, and how he had no concern for credit as a translator.

TYNDALE'S MARTYRDOM

The betrayal of Tyndale was by a supposed friend. Tyndale was at the time living with Thomas Poyntz, an English merchant in Antwerp. In May, 1535, Henry Phillips, to whom Tyndale had lent money, and to whom he had indeed given forty shillings that very morning, had Tyndale arrested as he was leaving the house to dine with a friend. Tyndale was taken to the Castle of Vilvorde near Brussels, where he was imprisoned for a year and 135 days. Cromwell made futile efforts on his behalf, and Poyntz also tried in vain to save Tyndale. Poyntz himself was arrested.

A century ago there was discovered in Belgium a letter written by Tyndale while he was in prison. It is in Latin and written to the

Marquis of Bergen, who was governor of the castle. In the letter Tyndale requests from the commissary some of his goods and a warmer cap, because, he writes, " I suffer greatly from cold in the head, and am afflicted by a perpetual catarrh, which is much increased in this cell." He also asks for a warmer coat, a piece of cloth to patch his leggings, and other garments. And he requests a lamp for use in the evening, for " it is indeed wearisome sitting alone in the dark." He writes that most of all he wants a Hebrew Bible, a Hebrew grammar, and a Hebrew dictionary, " that I may pass the time in that study." It would be difficult to illustrate more effectively the interest of Tyndale's life.

The trial, at which Tyndale acted as his own lawyer, ended with Tyndale condemned as a heretic. At his trial Tyndale maintained that faith alone justifies before God (*sola fides iustificat apud Deum*). He was formally stripped of his priestly status, and was handed over to the secular authorities for execution. According to the law, he was strangled and then burned. His often quoted last words were, " Lord, open the king of England's eyes." This was on the morning of October 6, 1536.

CHARACTERISTICS OF TYNDALE'S TRANSLATIONS

In translating the New Testament, Tyndale had among his helps Erasmus' second and third editions of the Greek text, the Vulgate, and Luther's German translation. Many phrases were shaped by Luther's translation. Tyndale was a competent Greek scholar, and he knew several other languages as well, including Latin, Hebrew, French, Spanish, Italian, and German. Tyndale did not use the Wycliffe Bible as a help. The style of the two is very different. The language of the first edition of the Wycliffe Bible was stilted and mechanical and somewhat comparable to the English of the interlinear translations (see p. 15), and even with the revisions of Purvey's edition it was still " translation English." By contrast, Tyndale's translation was in free, idiomatic English. It has had immense influence on subsequent translations, and is responsible for much of their beauty and excellence.

Much that we love in the King James Version is owed to Tyndale and is reflected also in the Revised Standard Version. To an extent exceeding that of the King James Version, and more especially the later English Revised Version and the American Standard Version, Tyndale's translation possessed a rich vocabulary, and he did not hesitate to vary his translation of the same Greek word if the context and the demands of effective English called for it. His translation was popular, not only because it was a good one, but because it was in language understood by the people. It has been estimated that one third of the King James Version of the New Testament is worded as Tyndale had it, and that even in the remaining two thirds the general literary structure set by Tyndale has been retained. Some scholars have said that ninety per cent of Tyndale is reproduced in the King James Version of the New Testament.

Luther A. Weigle, the chairman of the Standard Bible Committee which this year has issued the Revised Standard Version, comments that the English Bible owes more to Tyndale than to any other one man, not only because he was the first to translate into English from the Hebrew and Greek, but because the basic structure of his translation has endured through all subsequent changes (see L. A. Weigle, *The English New Testament from Tyndale to the Revised Standard Version,* Abingdon-Cokesbury Press, 1949). The Revised Standard Version of today is not a new translation, but a revision, and as a result of direct and indirect influence many of Tyndale's renderings have been retained. The revisers had before them not only the older authorized translations, but also Tyndale's translation. Some of the familiar phrases and sentences in the Revised Standard Version kept from Tyndale have been noted by Weigle. Among them are: " You cannot serve God and mammon " (Matt. 6:24); " Consider the lilies of the field, how they grow " (Matt. 6:28); " Where two or three are gathered in my name, there am I in the midst of them " (Matt. 18:20); " A prophet has no honor in his own country " (John 4:44); " It is more blessed to give than to receive " (Acts 20:35); " The unsearchable riches of Christ " (Eph. 3:8).

Among the things that Sir Thomas More had criticized in Tyndale's translation was the fact that Tyndale had " chaunged the name of charyte," i.e., that he had used the word " love " rather than the word " charity " to translate the Greek word *agape.* But Tyndale was correct in his rendering, and the later translations, from Coverdale in 1535 through the first edition of the Bishops' Bible in 1568, recognized this and followed Tyndale. Due to Latinizing influence, the second edition of the Bishops' Bible reverted to "charity" in thirty-two instances. The King James Version kept "charity" in twenty-six of these cases. The original preference for "charity" was due to its similarity to the Latin *caritas,* meaning "love," used in the Vulgate — this despite the fact that the word "charity" had obvious associations that did not make it as adequate a translation.

A Comparison

In this connection it is interesting to compare Tyndale's translation of I Cor. 13:1–4 with the earlier Wycliffe Bible, the later King James Version, and the Revised Standard Version. The Revised Standard Version, like the English Revised Version of 1881 and the American Standard Version of 1901, reads "love" instead of "charity." There was considerable outcry against the rendering "love" in this familiar passage when the English Revised Version appeared, the objection being based not on considerations of the proper translation, but on the familiarity of the passage. But sometimes the plain meaning of the original makes it necessary to change even familiar passages, and truth and not error should dominate in any adequate translation.

Wycliffe:
"If I speke with tungis of men and of aungels, and I haue not charite, I am made as bras sownynge or a cymbal tinkynge, and if I haue profecie, and knowe alle mysteries, and al kynnynge, and if I haue al feith so that I meue hillis fro her place and I haue not charite I am nou3ht, and if I departe alle my godis in to metis of pore men, and if I bitake my bodi so that I brenne, and I haue not charite it profetith to me no thing, charite is pacient, it is benyngne, charite enuyeth not, it doth not wickidli it is not blowun."

Tyndale:
"Though I spake with the tonges of men and angels, and yet had no love, I were even as soundinge brasse: or as a tynklynge Cymball.

And though I coulde prophesy, and vnderstode all secrets, and all knowledge: yee, yf I had all fayth so that I coulde move mountayns oute of ther places, and yet had no love, I were nothynge. And though I bestowed all my gooddes to fede the poore, and though I gave my body even that I burned, and yet had no love, it profeteth me nothinge. Love suffreth longe, and is corteous. Love envieth not. Love doth not frowardly, swelleth not."

King James Version:
"Though I speake with the tongues of men and of Angels, and haue not charity, I am become as sounding brasse or a tinkling cymbal. And though I haue the gift of prophesie, and vnderstand all mysteries and all knowledge: and though I haue all faith, so that I could remooue mountaines, and haue no charitie, I am nothing. And though I bestowe all my goods to feede the poore, and though I giue my body to bee burned, and haue not charitie, it profiteth me nothing. Charitie suffereth long, and is kinde: charitie enuieth not; charitie vaunteth not it selfe, is not puffed vp."

Revised Standard Version:
"If I speak in the tongues of men and of angels, but have not love, I am a noisy gong or a clanging cymbal. And if I have prophetic powers, and understand all mysteries and all knowledge, and if I have all faith, so as to remove mountains, but have not love, I am nothing. If I give away all that I have, and if I deliver my body to be burned, but have not love, I gain nothing. Love is patient and kind; love is not jealous or boastful; it is not arrogant or rude."

A glance shows how Tyndale's phraseology is different from that of the Wycliffe Bible but has contributed largely to the King James Version and to the Revised Standard Version. In v. 9 of this chapter Tyndale reads, "For oure knowledge is vnparfect, and oure prophesyinge is ynperfet," but the King James Version has, "For we know in part, and we prophesie in part." However, as a more happy rendering, the Revised Standard Version follows Tyndale, reading, "For our knowledge is imperfect and our prophecy is imperfect." On the other hand, the reader may see where in vs. 1–4 at a number of points the Revised Standard Version follows the King James

Version as over against Tyndale, and at some points has a reading differing from both, demanded by the original text or for clarity in translation.

Any translation becomes in part antiquated in time because of the archaisms it contains, as the language changes. Languages are not static. We in our day have seen new words come into our English language. Some words lose their common usage, and others change their meaning. There are more archaic words in Tyndale's Old Testament than in his New Testament. Among such words in the Pentateuch are almery (cupboard), bruterar (murmurer), comentye (congregation), daysmen (judges), fayre (gently), royalme (realm), seuerall (separate), tached (arrested), totehill (watchtower), tyllman (farmer), whote (hot), yerlee (early). Tyndale's translation is noted for its lack of stiffness and artificiality, and we find such lighthearted expressions as when Joseph in Gen. 39:2 is called " a luckie felowe," or when the serpent says to Eve, " Tush, ye shall not dye."

In trying to avoid the mechanical literalism and unnecessarily strict uniformities of the English Revised Version and the American Standard Version, and by revising " in the direction of the simple, classic . . . style of the King James Version," the translators of the Revised Standard Version were at the same time by virtue of this fact revising in the direction of Tyndale. We may use the first five verses from Genesis and a few verses from the story of Joseph (Gen. 37:4–8) to illustrate something of Tyndale's style in the Pentateuch. One can see in Tyndale's avoidance of the repetitious " and " at the beginning of vs. 2 and 3 in Gen., ch. 1, in his omission of " the face of " in v. 2, and in the structure of the last half of v. 5, something of his avoidance of literalism, and the resultant smooth and effective rendering.

Gen., ch. 1:
(1) (2) "In the begynnynge God created heaven and erth. The erth was voyde and emptie, ād darcknesse was vpon the depe,
(3) and the spirite of god moved vpon the water. Than God sayd:
(4) let there be lyghte and there was lyghte. And God sawe the lyghte that it was good: and devyded the lyghte from the darcknesse,

(5) and called the lyghte daye, and the darcknesse nyghte: and so of the evenynge and mornynge was made the fyrst daye."

Gen., ch. 37:

(4)   "When his brothren sawe that their father loued him more than all his brethern, they hated him and voude not speke one

(5) kynde worde vnto him. Moreouer Ioseph dreamed a dreame and tolde it his brethren: wherefore they hated him yet the

(6) more. And he sayde vnto them heare I praye yow this dreame

(7) which I haue dreamed: Beholde we were makynge sheues in the felde: and loo, my shefe arose and stode vp right, and youres

(8) stode rounde aboute and made obeysaunce to my shefe. Than sayde his brethren vnto him: what, shalt thou be oure kynge or shalt thou reigne ouer us? And they hated hī yet the more, because of his dreame and of his wordes."

III ✍

THE GENEALOGY OF THE KING JAMES VERSION

TRANSLATION IN THE TRADITION

THE later authorized versions of the Bible had their antecedents, as truly as does a person. No responsible translator of the Bible translates *de novo,* making a totally " original " translation, ignoring the suggestions and helps of earlier translations. This is even true of James Moffatt's translation of the Bible, despite the fact that it is an attempt to make a completely fresh translation rather than to revise older translations. It is particularly true of the translations of the Bible that are in any real sense authorized versions. The present Revised Standard Version is a revision of the American Standard Version of 1901 in the light of the best knowledge of today and " in the direction of the simple, classic English style of the King James Version."

The translators of the King James Version indicate their dependence in the preface to their translation, saying, " Yet for all that, as nothing is begun and perfited at the same time, and the later thoughts are thought to be the wiser: so, if we building vpon their foundation that went before vs, and being holpen by their labours, doe endeuour to make that better which they left so good; no man, we are sure, hath cause to mislike us; they, we perswade our selues, if they were aliue, would thank us." The King James Bible was a deliberate revision of the preceding Bishops' Bible, which was itself a revision. The versions " in the tradition " are actually revisions of revisions. For this reason, we may speak of the genealogy or the ancestry of the English Bible, and we have called Tyndale the " father " of our English Bible.

MILES COVERDALE

We begin with Miles Coverdale, who was responsible for two versions of our English Bible. Miles Coverdale was born in 1488 in the district of Coverdale in Yorkshire. He was thus a contemporary of Tyndale, although he made his most important version after Tyndale's death. He went to Cambridge, where he studied philosophy and theology. He was admitted to the priesthood in 1514, and entered the monastery of the Austin Friars which was at Cambridge. Something of the theological atmosphere of this monastery may be gathered from the fact that its prior, Robert Barnes, had helped to circulate Tyndale's New Testament. Barnes was also reported to have likened the New Testament in Latin to a "cymball tynnklyng and brasse soundyng." After Barnes preached against the luxury of Cardinal Wolsey, he was summoned to meet a charge of heresy, and Coverdale went with him to help him to prepare his defense. Although Barnes yielded at this time and did penance by casting fagots on heretical books to be burned, he later relented and was sentenced to be burned at the stake. He managed to flee to the Continent, but he eventually met his death as a martyr in 1540.

After a while Coverdale gave up his monastic habit to devote himself to evangelical preaching. As a reformer he was less virulent than Tyndale, and he did not arouse the strong antagonisms that Tyndale engendered. He was a more quiet and less passionate person, who preferred to reform from within, and partly for this reason he escaped the martyrdom that came to Tyndale. He had powerful friends, under whose patronage he may have prepared his translation of the Bible. One of these was Sir Thomas More, at whose home he had been an occasional visitor. The other was Thomas Cromwell, who was to become vicegerent for King Henry VIII in ecclesiastical affairs and was entrusted with the suppression of the monasteries. In his preaching Coverdale opposed the confessional and the worship of images.

Coverdale was living on the continent of Europe for most of the period from 1528 to 1534, engaged in the translation of the Bible. A dubious report has Coverdale at Hamburg working with Tyndale on the translation of the Pentateuch in 1529. A royal proclamation in 1530 condemned Tyndale's writings and his New Testament, but in the same month a "bill in Englisshe to be published by the prechours" gave the information that King Henry had said he would cause the New Testament to be translated by learned men into English. Later in the year Latimer, bishop of Worcester, reminded the king of his promise, and in 1534 a convocation asked Thomas Cranmer, archbishop of Canterbury, to request the king to decree that the Scriptures be translated by certain honest and learned men named by the king. The times were obviously ripe for a translation that would be acceptable to the authorities. An attempt to have the bishops make a translation failed. Coverdale had his translation ready, and so, doubtless with the encouragement of Thomas Cromwell, he issued on October 4, 1535, what was the first printed English translation of the complete Bible.

COVERDALE'S BIBLE

It is uncertain where Coverdale's Bible was printed, but it was probably at Marburg, Germany, although many think it was at Zurich, Switzerland. Attractive wood-block illustrations surround the title page, and six woodcuts showing the days of creation introduce the reader pictorially to Genesis. There are a total of sixty-eight such separate wood blocks used to illustrate the volume, some used more than once, to make a total of 188 separate pictures. We may take them as a prototype or forerunner of our modern visual aids! The volume also had a map, oriented with the south at the top, and a comparison with the maps in *The Westminster Historical Atlas to the Bible* (1945) suggests how far cartography or map making and historical geography have developed since those days.

The original imprint gave the title as *BIBLIA, The Bible, that is, the holy Scripture of the Olde and New Testament, faithfully and truly translated out of Douche and Latyn in to Englishe.* In the same year, 1535, unbound sheets were brought to England and provided with a substitute title page, and the title omitted the clause "truly translated out of Douche and Latyn." This was doubtless because the "Douche" (i.e., German) referred to was Luther's translation, which might be looked upon as heretical, and perhaps so that it would not appear so obviously to be a translation of earlier translations. It may have been at this time that there were added several preliminary pages, a dedication "vnto the most victorious Prynce, and oure most gracyous Soueraigne Lorde, Kynge Henry the eyght," called "An Epistle vnto the Kynges hyghnesse," signed "youre graces humble subjecte and daylye oratour, Myles Couerdale." It contains fulsome praise of Henry, and the pope is denounced as the "blynde bysshoppe of Rome (that blynde Baalam)" and "that Antychrist of Rome," the "vntollerable and nomore to be suffred abhominacions" he has caused being due to ignorance of Scripture. Despite this dedication, the Coverdale Bible did not have royal authority, although a corrected edition in 1537 carried the words "sett forth with the Kynges moost gracious licence." There exist today 120 copies of the Coverdale Bible.

Coverdale's Bible was not an original piece of work. The Old Testament was based chiefly on the Swiss-German version published in Zurich in 1524–1529, although Coverdale used extensively Tyndale's translation of the Pentateuch. The New Testament was a revision of Tyndale's New Testament compared with that of Luther. Coverdale also used the Latin Vulgate, as well as a Latin translation of 1528. The translation includes the Apocrypha. The title page of the section containing the Apocrypha has the subtitle, "The bokes and treatises which amonge the fathers of olde are not rekened to be of like authorite with the other bokes of the byble, nether are they foūde in the Canon of the Hebrue." In "A Prologe, Myles Couerdale vnto the Christen Reader," Coverdale's beginning statement illustrates the modesty so characteristic of him: "Considerynge how excellent knowlege and lernynge an interpreter of scripture oughte to haue in the tongues, and ponderyng also myne owne insufficiency therin, how weake I am to perfourme ye office of a translatoure, I was the more lothe to medle with this worke." He calls to mind the adversity of those who would have completed what they began, "if they had not had impediment," an obvious reference to the imprisonment of Tyndale, who was at the time in the Castle of Vilvorde.

Although it was a secondary translation, Coverdale's Bible possessed real qualities which made it influential in later translations, and some of the literary virtues of the King James, particularly in the books of poetry and the Prophets, are due to Coverdale's influence. Weigle points out (*Religion and Life,* 1946, p. 171) that to the Coverdale Bible are owed such phrases still preserved in the Revised Standard Version as "till heaven and earth pass away" (Matt. 5:18); "none of us lives to himself, and none of us dies to himself" (Rom. 14:7); "death is swallowed up in victory" (I Cor. 15:54), etc.

We shall return to Coverdale again. Not only did he print, in 1538, the Vulgate with a literal English translation and the Latin in parallel columns in order to show how the New Testament in English did not misrepresent the Vulgate, but he was to be largely responsible for another one of the significant translations "in the tradition." But more of that shortly.

John Rogers and "Matthew's Bible"

It was to no small extent due to John Rogers that the excellent qualities of Tyndale's translation of Scripture were incorporated in the stream of the more or less "official" translations of the Bible. John Rogers had graduated from Cambridge in 1525. He later went to the Continent to Antwerp to become chaplain to the "Merchant Adventurers." Here he met Tyndale. He became an energetic reformer and a disciple of Tyndale. He married a girl named Andriana Pratt, said to have been "more richly endowed with virtue and soberness of life than with worldly treasures," and by her he had eleven children. He was for a time pastor at Wittenberg. In 1537 he published, probably at Antwerp, the version known as "Matthew's Bible," Rogers taking the pen name of Thomas Matthew. It was a composite work, consisting of the translations of Tyndale and Coverdale. The New Testament is Tyndale's 1535 translation, and the Pentateuch is also Tyndale's translation. The books from Joshua through II Chronicles should also doubtless be ascribed to Tyndale, having been left unpublished by Tyndale at his death, as we have seen. The Apocrypha is Coverdale's translation, as also the books from Ezra to Malachi. Thus two thirds of Matthew's Bible was Tyndale's work. Because of this, and in contrast with Coverdale's Bible, Matthew's Bible was largely a translation from original tongues.

Matthew's Bible, along with chapter summaries, woodcuts, and marginal notes, contained at the beginning a concordance-dictionary, arranged alphabetically. It filled twenty-six pages, and was chiefly a translation of a concordance in the French Bible of Olivétan, a relative of Calvin. It is described as a "table of pryncypal matters conteyned in the Byble, in which the readers may fynde and practyse many commune places." It was naturally antipapal in sentiment, and we can see, for instance, a criticism of the Catholic view of "merit" in the discussion under "Meryte," where we read: "In lokynge ouer the Byble, as well the newe as the olde Testament, I haue not found this word meryte. Meryte then is nothynge," etc.

Matthew's Bible was dedicated to "Prynce Kyng Henry the Eyght and Queen Jane." Richard Grafton, "citizen and grocer," who had invested money in the version, sent a copy of it to Cranmer, archbishop of Canterbury, and Cranmer wrote to Thomas Cromwell and said, "So farre as I haue redde therof I like it better than any other translation hertofore made," and he asked him to show the book to the king and "obteign of his Grace, if you can, a license that the same may be sold and redde of euery person, withoute danger of any acte, proclamacion, or ordinaunce hertofore graunted to the contrary, vntill such a tyme that we, the Bishops, shall set forth a better translacion, which I thinke will not be till a day after domesday." The king agreed to Cranmer's request, and a royal proclamation was issued that the Bible being translated into the mother tongue should be taught by the curates and "openly laid forth in every parish church." It is a curious turn of circumstance that this translation, largely the work of one who had been burned as a heretic (i.e., Tyndale), should thus have received ecclesiastical and royal recognition.

Rogers himself died a martyr's death. He had returned to England after the death of Henry VIII, when Edward VI became king. But when Edward died and Queen Mary ascended the throne, the Catholics were back in power and relationships with Rome were re-established. Rogers was ordered to keep to his house, and in 1555 was brought to trial. At his trial he maintained that the pope had no more authority than other bishops. It was a foregone conclusion that he would be condemned to the stake. When he was awakened one morning and told that on that day he would be burned at the stake, he said quietly, " Then I need not tye my points." On the way to the place of execution he met his wife and eleven children, the youngest but a child at breast. The French ambassador reported that Rogers' children so comforted him that it seemed as if he were being led to a wedding. Of him as of others in this period we may say that " the blood of the martyrs is the seed of the Church."

The Great Bible

Matthew's (i.e., Rogers') Bible had been licensed by the king in 1537. But in the same year Coverdale's Bible, " newly ouersene and corrected," had been issued "with the Kynges moost gracious licence." To have two such widely variant translations circulating with authority was confusing, to say the least. It would put a weapon in the hands of those who were antagonistic toward a translation in the vernacular. This was especially true in view of the fact that one of the versions was largely the work of the heretic Tyndale, whose initials were actually at the end of the Old Testament section of that version! So Coverdale was asked by Thomas Cromwell to undertake the preparation of another version, based on Matthew's Bible, which would replace both it and Coverdale's own Bible. It is characteristic of the earnestness and lack of pretense of Coverdale that he agreed to do this. In fact, in the dedication to the Coverdale Bible, Coverdale had said that if anything in his translation was " translated amysse (for in many thynges we fayle euen when we thynke to be sure)," it was in the king's hand to correct, emend, or improve it, " yee and cleane to reiecte it," if in his godly wisdom he thought it necessary. In the dedication to his Latin-English New Testament mentioned above he had indicated that he was " alwaye wyllynge and ready to do my best aswel in one translation, as in another."

This new version which Coverdale now produced was called the Great Bible. It was a large-folio edition, and was issued in 1539. Perhaps because of lack of adequate press for such a project in England, and in order to secure better paper and a supply of experienced workmen, it was decided to do the printing in Paris. Because of an order of confiscation from the Inquisition, Coverdale, along with

Grafton who had accompanied him to Paris, had to flee from Paris, and the printer, Regnault, was arrested. Cromwell then had the type, presses, and workmen brought from Paris, and the printing was completed in London. Grafton and Whitchurch were the printers. According to the imprint at the end, it was " fynisshed " in April, 1539, but it was probably near the end of the year before the work was really completed.

It is deservedly called the Great Bible, for the pages of the 1539 edition measured 16½ by 11 inches. Both the quality of the paper and the artistry of the print (typography) merit high praise. There is a remarkable title page woodcut. At the top the enthroned King Henry is pictured handing a Bible to Archbishop Cranmer, who heads a clergy group at his left, and giving another copy to Thomas Cromwell, who stands before a group of nobility on his right. God is in the clouds above. On one side of the title Cranmer presents a copy of the Bible to a kneeling priest, while on the other Cromwell gives a copy to one of a group of nobility. Below a priest preaches to a crowd of commoners, while opposite him some men, perhaps those who would not acknowledge Henry's authority, peer through the barred windows of Newgate Prison. Wavy ribbonlike bands carry the words of the various personages. As Willoughby remarks in his description of the scenes, the engraving dramatizes the patriotic and religious loyalty which Henry, Cranmer, and Cromwell hoped might result from making the Bible available to the people in the vernacular.

It was thus a revision of the Matthew's Bible. In making the revision, for the New Testament Coverdale had consulted the Latin text of Erasmus and the Vulgate, and for the Old Testament had made use of a new literal Latin translation from the Hebrew by Münster. Because of his use of more recent authorities who were conversant with the original tongues, he was able to indicate on the title page that it was translated " after the veryte of the Hebrue and Greke textes by ye dylygent studye of dyuerse excellent learned men." It has been suggested that the translation was made by indicating the changes on a copy of Matthew's Bible, even as the translators of the King James Version are reputed to have annotated a copy of the Bishops' Bible. The year after it was issued, a revision of the Great Bible was made, and a preface added to it by Archbishop Cranmer.

A new era seemed to have entered, although it was not to last very long. The Great Bible became *the* authorized version. It has with reason been called the first authorized English Bible. The king had turned the Great Bible over to Bishop Gardiner and others for judgment, and they had tried to hinder its publication because of what they thought to be its faults. But when they could not point out to the king any heresies, King Henry said, " If there be no heresies, then, in God's name, let it go abroad among our people." The 1540 revision of the Great Bible bore on the title page the words, " This is the Byble apoynted to the use of the churches," and in May, 1541, the king issued a proclamation " for the Byble of the largest and greatest volume to be had in euery church." Archbishop Lee of York ordered all curates to provide a Bible within forty days, and have it chained in some open place in the church. The people gathered around Bibles thus placed in the churches, eager to read them, and they even read during the church services and while the sermons were being preached, some arguing so loudly that they had to be admonished. Three editions of the Great Bible were published in 1540, and three in 1541.

The April, 1540, edition of the Great Bible, which was the second edition, and the subsequent editions carried an important preface written by Archbishop Cranmer and called by Willoughby a primary document of the English Reformation. It is because of this preface that the Great Bible is often spoken of as Cranmer's Bible. In the preface Cranmer writes " for two sondrye sortes of people," i.e., in order that the book may be better accepted by those " which hitherto coulde not well beare it," and that it may better be used by those " which hertofore haue mysused it." He protests against those who refuse to hear or read the Scriptures " in theyr vulgar tonges " and who discourage others from reading and hearing the Scriptures. He criticizes those who slander and hinder the Word of God by " theyr inordinate readyng, undiscrete speakyng, contentious disputyng, or otherwise by theyr licencyous lyuinge." In his opposition to those who are merely content with that to which they are accustomed, he recalls an " olde prouerbe " that after the discovery of the cultivation

of grain many continued to delight in malt and acorns, rather than
eat bread made of good grain. The bearing of this on the reception
of the translated Bible is obvious, and not without its application
today. Cranmer appeals to the history of the Church for support
for the Bible in the vernacular. He thinks that in the Bible men,
women, young, old, learned, unlearned, rich, poor, priests, laymen,
lords, ladies, officers, tenants, and mean men, virgins, wives, widows,
lawyers, merchants, artificers, farmers, and all manner of persons
may learn all things they ought to believe, what they should do and
not do, "aswell concerning almyghtye God as also concernynge
them selues and all other."

TAVERNER'S BIBLE

A translation of the Bible more important than is usually recognized was made by a layman, Richard Taverner. He was a protégé
of Thomas Cromwell. He became a lawyer and was appointed clerk
of the king's signet. The year following the death of Cromwell he
was for a short time imprisoned in the Tower of London. He was
licensed as a lay preacher, and even preached before the king. His
literary works were many, but he is best known for his translation
of the Bible issued in 1539 and dedicated to Henry VIII. Taverner's
Bible was a revision of Matthew's Bible of 1537. His revision of the
New Testament was the most important part, for he was an excellent Greek scholar. The Old Testament revision was little more than
a correction of the English with reference to the Latin of the Vulgate. Professors Hutson and Willoughby have recently shown that
Taverner's Bible is more important than has generally been thought.
It influenced the 1582 Catholic translation of the New Testament,
which in turn was consulted by the King James Version translators.
By this means an appreciable number of Taverner's readings have
come down into the King James Version. In the dedication Taverner
comments on the difficulty of a single person producing a translation in a short time, and suggests that an adequate translation would
require a deeper conferring together of many learned scholars and a
longer time.

FORCES OF OPPOSITION

In a convocation in 1542 the bishops planned to make a revision "according to that Bible which is commonly read in the English Church," i.e., the Vulgate. Bishop Gardiner prepared a list of ninety-nine Latin words which "for their genuine and native meaning and for the majesty of their matter" he thought should be kept in the proposed revision, or at least turned into English as closely as possible. Among the words he suggested were such words as *poenitentia, pontifex, ancilla, baptizare, sandalium, lites, simulachrum, panis propositionis, concupiscentia, peccatum, inenarrabilis, didrachma, charitas, distribueretur, impositio manuum,* etc. It was fortunate that nothing came of this attempt to Latinize the Bible for the benefit of the clergy. The project fell through, Cranmer being largely responsible for "putting the skids under it," and, as Eadie says, no further attempt was made to papalize the translation and put a foreign mask on its everyday English.

Indicative of the fears in the minds of many of the authorities, an act passed by parliament in 1543 prohibited reading Tyndale's translation, and decreed that "no manner of persons, after the first of October, should take upon them to read openly to others in any church or open assembly, within any of the king's dominions, the Bible or any part of the Scripture in English, unless he was so appointed thereunto by the king, or by any ordinary, on pain of suffering 100 months' imprisonment . . . every nobleman and gentlewoman, being a householder, may read or cause to be read by any of his own family, servants in his house, orchard, or garden, to his own family, any text of the Bible; and also every merchantman, being a householder, and any other persons, other than women, apprentices, etc., might read to themselves privately the Bible. But no women, except noblewomen and gentlewomen, might read to themselves alone; and no artificers, apprentices, journeymen, servingmen of the degrees of yeomen, husbandmen, or labourers, were to read the New Testament to themselves or to any other, privately or openly, on pain of one month's imprisonment." If ever there was class legislation, this is it. One does not have to guess how the Carpenter of Nazareth would have reacted to it. Other decrees of

King Henry were even more restrictive, but when he died and Edward VI came to the throne, the situation improved. It was ordered that within three months curates should set up " Bibles in large volume," and every parson, vicar, curate, etc., under the degree of bachelor of divinity should possess his own New Testament in Latin and English.

COVERDALE'S LATER LIFE

Thomas Cromwell, Coverdale's friend and patron, had urged further reforms in the Church at the time when King Henry was on the side of doctrinal conservatism and when parliament in 1539 passed the Six Articles, which reaffirmed the faith though they did make clear the break with Rome. Cromwell further gained the displeasure of Henry because he urged on Henry marriage to the unattractive Anne of Cleves, " the Flanders mare," Henry's fourth wife, to cement a Protestant alliance on the Continent. Henry now had no use for Cromwell, and had his head chopped off on July 28, 1540. That same year Coverdale found it wise to leave England. He spent some time in Tübingen, and was pastor and schoolmaster in Bavaria at Bergzabern. He married Elizabeth Macheson, a sister-in-law of Joannes MacAlpinus, who had taken part in the first translation of the Bible into Danish. The year following Henry's death, Coverdale returned to England and became chaplain to King Edward VI. In 1551 he was consecrated as bishop. In this period he published a number of works. When Edward died and Catholic Queen Mary succeeded to the throne, the time was one of terror and torture for the Protestants. Under Heath, the successor of Gardiner as Mary's lord chancellor, 217 persons are said to have suffered martyrdom, and during Mary's reign 400 persons lost their lives by imprisonment, torture, and burning at the stake. Among them were John Rogers and Archbishop Cranmer. Cranmer had at first submitted and had signed a recantation, but with last-minute courage he had declared again his Protestant faith. At the stake he held in the flame, until it was consumed, the hand that had signed the retraction. Even the printing of Bible verses in English on the walls of the churches was strictly forbidden.

Coverdale was made a prisoner at large, and he might have been a martyr had not his wife's brother-in-law MacAlpinus persuaded Christian III, king of Denmark, to intercede on his behalf. It took two letters from King Christian, and then Coverdale was reluctantly permitted to leave England for Denmark. We find him later preaching for a while in Westphalia. From there he moved to Bergzabern to take up again his pastorate there, and he also went to Geneva. He returned to England at the accession of Elizabeth as queen. In 1563 he caught the plague, but recovered. He was appointed to the living of St. Magnus, near London Bridge, but we find him practically penniless in his old age, despite recognitions that he was given in academic circles. He resigned his charge in 1566, but continued to preach as occasion offered. At the age of eighty-one he died. We must acclaim him as one of the great figures in the history of the English Bible. He may not have been so courageously aggressive as Tyndale and Rogers, and his work did not possess the originality of some others in the history of the English Bible, for he leaned on secondary sources. Yet we should not underestimate his scholarship or his influence.

THE GENEVAN BIBLE

After the Great Bible there were yet to be two significant limbs on the genealogical tree of the King James Version. These were the Genevan Bible and the Bishops' Bible. Many Protestants had fled from England in the face of the fanatical terrorism of Queen Mary's reign. Among these were five bishops, five deans, and fifty eminent clergymen. Dissensions arose at Frankfort, among the exiles there, over questions of clerical vestments and the church service. The more nonconforming section of them went to Geneva, Switzerland, a city closely connected with Biblical scholarship and numerous Bible translations. There Olivétan had translated the French Bible, the standard version for French Protestants (1535). The exiles engaged in Bible translation. William Whittingham, a brother-in-law of Calvin, edited and published the New Testament in 1557. But the more important fruit of the labors of the English scholars in Geneva was the Genevan Bible, published in April, 1560, and dedicated to Queen Elizabeth, with admonitions to her to " root out and cut down these weeds and impediments [i.e., the Catholic adherents of the pope] . . . in imitation of the noble Josias who destroyed not only their idols and appurtenances, but also burnt the priests' bones upon their altars," etc. Although some think he did, Coverdale had no part in making the Genevan Bible. When the exiles returned at the accession of Elizabeth, Whittingham and one or two others stayed at Geneva to see the work finished. In the preface the translators point out that " considering the infancie of those tymes and imperfect knollage of the tongues, in respect of this ripe age and cleare light which God hath now reueiled, the [older] translations required greatly to be perused and reformed."

The title of the Genevan Bible indicated that it was " translated according to the Ebrue and Greke, and conferred with the best translations in divers languages. With moste profitable annotations upon all the harde places, and other thinges of great importance as may appeare in the Epistle to the Reader." The chief changes in the Old Testament were in those books which Tyndale had not translated, and which had to be made to accord with the Hebrew rather than the Latin. In the New Testament the revisers consulted the Latin translation and commentary of Beza, the most famous Biblical scholar of the time, whose home was in Geneva. The Genevan Bible was the first complete English translation of the Bible to be divided into verses. One of the several things that endeared this version to the readers was the marginal notes, indicating variant translations, the more literal Hebrew, the passages most profitably memorized, the " principal matters," and annotations on all the hard places and obscure words. There were also added " certyne mappes of Cosmographie " and two tables, one giving the interpretation of Hebrew names and the other containing " all the chefe and principal matters of the whole Bible," alphabetically arranged.

The popularity of the Genevan Bible was increased by the fact that it was printed in simple Roman type and was a smaller (quarto) size than the previous Bibles " of larger volume." As Eadie comments, it became at once the people's book in England and Scotland. The Genevan Bible was the first Bible to be published in Scotland. An act of parliament in Scotland required " every householder worth 300 merks of yearly rent, and every yeoman or burgess worth £500 stock was to have a Bible and Psalm Book in the vulgar language, under penalty of ten pounds." Searchers were designated to visit all dwellings and report whether or not they possessed a Bible.

The Genevan Bible was the cherished volume in all the Puritan households, and was the Bible of our Pilgrim Fathers. This despite the fact that it was not authorized for use in the churches, for the Great Bible held this position. The Bishops' Bible which was to follow was not able to supplant it, and for a while it held its own against the King James Version. Its persistent influence is dramatically illustrated by the fact that the preface to the King James Version quotes from the Genevan Bible, not from the King James Version itself. There were to be some 140 editions of the Genevan Bible printed. It is often called the "Breeches Bible," for the translation of Gen. 3:7 reads, "They sewed fig tree leaves together and made themselves breeches."

We in our day are familiar with Soldiers' Bibles, distributed to men in the armed forces. The earliest known Soldiers' Bible was the Cromwellian Short Bible, of 1643, called "The Souldiers Pocket Bible," compiled by Edmund Calamy to meet the religious needs of Oliver Cromwell's army. It contained 125 verses, all but seven of them from the Old Testament. All but one of them are taken from the Genevan Bible. It was later reprinted as "The Christian Soldier's Penny Bible" in 1693 in the King James Version, with thirty verses added and the captions modified.

From the Genevan Bible there have come down into today's Revised Standard Version such expressions as "recovering of sight to the blind" (Luke 4:18); "in all these things we are more than conquerors through him who loved us" (Rom. 8:37); "we have the mind of Christ" (I Cor. 2:16); and "so great a cloud of witnesses" (Heb. 12:1) (Weigle, *Religion in Life,* 1946, p. 171).

THE BISHOPS' BIBLE

The latest predecessor of the King James Version was the Bishops' Bible. The bishops or other clergy in England had no hand in the origin of the Genevan Bible, and it came to be identified with the more liberal party. So Matthew Parker, archbishop of Canterbury, instigated a revision of the Great Bible, with the bishops and other learned men to take part in the work. The archbishop was to assign various parts of the Bible to the different translators, himself putting the final touches on the translation and seeing to the publishing. Except where the Hebrew and Greek original demanded revision, the reading of the Great Bible was retained.

It required four years to complete the revision, and a bound copy was presented to Queen Elizabeth upon its completion in 1568. It contained 123 engravings of maps, pictures, and coats of arms. At the end of the title were the words, " *Cum Privilegio Regiae Majestatis,*" but no royal confirmation was actually given to it. In 1577 an edition appeared with the words, " Set forth by authoritie," i.e., the authority of the bishops. Convocation made enactments on behalf of the translation, and each bishop and archbishop was ordered to have in his house a copy of the Bible " of the largest volume, as lately printed in London," placed in the hall or dining room where it would be useful to servants or to strangers. The order applied also to each cathedral, and likewise to all churches so far as could conveniently be done.

From the Bishops' Bible there have come down into the Revised Standard Version such familiar expressions as " persecuted for righteousness' sake " (Matt. 5:10); " faithless and perverse generation " (Matt. 17:17), and " overcome evil with good " (Rom. 12:21).

The Rheims and Douai Bible

The popularity of the English Bible among the Protestants put the Catholics on the defensive, where they felt they had to protect themselves by providing an English translation of their own. It was thus that with hesitancy and lack of conviction as to its propriety there was issued the so-called Rheims and Douai Version. The New Testament was issued in 1582 by the English college in Rheims, France. The Old Testament was published in 1609–1610 in Douai, Flanders, by the English college, which had moved back there from Rheims. In the preface to the New Testament it was stated that it was published, not because of the erroneous opinion that the Scriptures should of necessity always be in the mother tongue, " or that they ought, or were ordained by God, to be read indifferently of all, or could be easily vnderstood of euery one that readeth or heareth them in a knowen language." It was admonished that one should not assume that translated Bibles used to be in the hands of every " husbandman, artificer, prentice, boies, girles, mistresse, maide, man," or were for " table talke, for alebenches, for boates and barges, and for euery prophane person and companie. No, in those better times men were neither so il nor so curious of themselues, so to abuse the blessed booke of Christ." For this reason the preface to the King James Version of 1611 affirmed that the Church of Rome allowed her children the Scriptures in the mother tongue as " a gift, not deseruing to be called a gift, an vnprophitable gift. . . . Yea, so vnwilling they are to communicate the Scriptures to the peoples vnderstanding in any sort, that they are not ashamed to confesse that wee forced them to translate it into English against their wills."

The Rheims and Douai Bible was a translation from the Vulgate, and, despite its Latinized style and ecclesiastical vocabulary, it does have its virtues. In the New Testament the Greek was also consulted. It was accompanied by a commentary to present to the reader the proper Catholic interpretation and teachings. The total contribution it makes in the history of the English Bible, however, is slight, even though some of its phrases were used by the King James Version translators. Originating from it and carried on down through the King James Version into the present Revised Standard Version are: " Owe no one anything " (Rom. 13:8); " Why, what evil has he done? " (Matt. 27:23); " To me to live is Christ, and to die is gain " (Phil. 1:21). Naturally such a reading as, " Behold I will screake under you as a wayne screaketh loden with hay " in Amos 2:13 was not adopted! The Rheims and Douai Version was revised by Bishop Challoner in 1750, and this has been the best-known Catholic version in English down to the present century. It was made the approved English version for Catholics in America in 1810.

REFORMATION, OLD AND NEW

Our own time recalls that of the sixteenth century, when so many of the translations of the Bible described in these pages were made. Most of these translations were part and parcel of the spirit of the Reformation. A number of the translations made in our day cannot be separated from the spirit of ecumenicity or church unity now in the air, as we seem to be in the midst of a new Reformation.

IV ⚜

THE KING JAMES VERSION

THE KING JAMES VERSION IN PERSPECTIVE

THE King James Version has become so sanctified by time and use that to many people it has come to be regarded as *the* Bible. It is not always realized that people who speak a different language have the Bible translated in their own vernacular tongue, so that there are many widely used translations in many different languages, of which the King James Version is but one. The King James Version is what it is to a large extent because of the manner in which it incorporated within itself that which had been found excellent in earlier translations. To some the King James Version is the original Bible, and problems of translation from original Hebrew and Greek manuscripts are unknown to them. They take an attitude toward it that is somewhat comparable to that taken toward the Latin Vulgate by the medieval Roman Church. Shortly after the publication of the Revised Standard Version of the New Testament in February, 1946, a woman remarked to one of the translators that she liked it almost as well as the Bible! She meant by this, of course, the King James Version.

All this is understandable, and rather than be negatively critical of such attitudes we should take them as a tribute to the King James Version. The King James Version had within it those excellent qualities which caused it to supplant effectively the earlier translations which we now think of as only stages in the development of the English Bible and as objects of historical interest in museums and private collections. And as yet, although they have been widely used, subsequent translations have not replaced the King James Version in the affections of the people or in private and public use.

What the future holds cannot be predicted. In our day, particularly, no royal decree or ecclesiastical convocation can give a translation ultimate authority; it must commend itself to both the heart and the mind of the worshiper. And we may be certain that any version that so commends itself must contain the virtues of the King James Version, incorporating within itself that which the centuries since 1611 have tested. It is not enough to recognize the changes that have occurred in the English language which make some of the vocabulary of the King James Version subject to misunderstanding, nor is it sufficient merely to use more authoritative original manuscripts, or to employ our increased knowledge of the original tongues. There is that in the King James Version which is too worthy to become a curio for scholars, a mere monument in the history of English literature, a reference in libraries.

KING JAMES THE FIRST

The dedication beginning, "TO THE MOST HIGH AND MIGHTIE Prince, Iames by the grace of God King of Great Britaine, France and Ireland, Defender of the Faith, &c. THE TRANSLATORS OF THE BIBLE wish Grace, Mercie, and Peace, through Iesvs Christ our Lord," is still printed in our Bibles, with the spelling modernized. But few read the dedication or know anything about this king. The dedication or "Epistle Dedicatorie" describes James as enriched by God's heavenly hand with many singular and extraordinary graces, and expresses the hope that he may be "the wonder of the world in this later age, for happinesse and true felicitie." James was a man of extraordinary talents, contradictory impulses, and unaccountable likings. A recent biography of him is subtitled "The Wisest Fool in Christendom." He was not an inconsiderable literary figure, and his astounding knowledge of Scripture is reflected in his writings on political theory, poetry, theology, and the Bible. While not yet twenty years old he wrote a "Paraphrase on the Revelation of St. John."

James believed in the divine right of kings, and held that this right was hereditary, and that the king was responsible to God alone, and not to his subjects. As "Defender of the Faith" and head of the State Church, he came into opposition with the Puritans on the one hand and the Catholics and their papal claims on the other. In his struggles with both he was motivated by a combination of religious and political considerations. In the dedication the translators speak of being " traduced by Popish persons at home or abroad," and of being " maligned by selfe-conceited brethren, who runne their owne wayes." King James's dislike of the Puritans was because of their objection to his views of kingship and his claim to be " supreme Governour in causes Ecclesiasticall." He said of the Puritans, " I will make them conform, or I will harry them out of the land, or yet do worse."

THE BEGINNINGS OF THE KING JAMES VERSION

James had been King James VI of Scotland, and he came down to England in 1603 to become the successor of Elizabeth. On his way to London he was presented with the " Millenary Petition," containing about a thousand signatures and for this reason bearing this name. The petition was a statement of the grievances of the Puritan-minded clergy toward the Church. As a result, the Hampton Court Conference was called in January, 1604, for the purpose of hearing and determining " things said to be amiss in the church." From the viewpoint of the Puritans who were seeking reform, the conference was a failure. But the fruits of the conference were to be far-reaching, for the King James Version was to result from it.

When the conference had failed of its purpose, President John Reynolds, of Corpus Christi College at Oxford, an outstanding Puritan, moved the king that there might be a new translation of the Bible, because those which were " allowed in the raignes of Henrie the eight and Edward the sixt were corrupt and not aunswerable to the truth of the Originall." The bishop of London objected, saying that if every man's humor were followed there would be no end to translating. Consonant with his deep interest in Scripture, the king immediately gave the idea his warm support. He cautioned against having marginal notes, since he had found those in the Genevan Bible very partial, untrue, seditious, dangerous, and even permitting disobedience to kings. Naturally the Puritan flavor of the Genevan Bible was obnoxious to the king and contrary to his idea of absolute royal sovereignty.

In the preface to the King James Version, "The Translators to the Reader," there is a reference to the "importunate petitions of the Puritanes" at the Hampton Court Conference, and the statement that when force of reason had defeated the Puritans, as a last resort they objected to the "Communion booke, since it maintained the Bible as it was there translated, which was as they said, a most corrupted translation. And although this was judged to be but a very poore and emptie shift; yet euen hereupon did his Maiestie beginne to bethinke himselfe of the good that might ensue by a new translation, and presently after gaue order for this Translation which is now presented vnto thee." We may be sure that the clergy for the most part had little desire for a new translation, and so it is to the "Puritanes" among them, and more particularly to James, that ultimately the translation was owed.

TRANSLATION PROCEDURES

The king mentions his appointment of fifty-four scholars to do the translating, although the names of only forty-seven appear in the records. They were from Oxford University, Cambridge University, and Westminster. The translation was a Church of England version, and there were no nonconformists on the committee, although it did include some Puritan-minded clergy. President Reynolds, who had made the original suggestion, was among those appointed for the translating of the Bible, although he died in 1607, the year the work started.

The royal treasury was empty, and Bishop Bancroft of London was asked by the king to appeal to the bishops and the clergy to contribute to the expenses of the translation, but apparently nothing came of it. King James advised ecclesiastical preferment for the translators, suggesting that they be promoted to vacancies that might occur, and later some were made bishops or given other advances. The translators were divided into six companies, two meeting at Westminster, two at Oxford, and two at Cambridge. They were entertained free of charge at the universities, eating at the college tables. But, as Eadie says, the King James Version never cost King James a farthing, and, as another scholar says, James provided only enthusiasm. But he did supply this, and his interest was so great that Bishop Bancroft was persuaded that James rejoiced more in the translation than in the peace just concluded with Spain, and that he was ready of his most princely disposition to have borne the expenses, but some of the lords did not hold it convenient.

The work was formally begun in 1607, although preceded by private work by the translators, and it was finished in 1611. The various companies did different parts of the Bible; for instance, one of the Oxford companies did the Major and Minor Prophets and the book of Lamentations, and the other Oxford company did the Gospels, The Acts, and Revelation. Specific rules were set to guide the committees. Among them we may mention the following: The Bishops' Bible was to be followed and as little altered as the "truth of the original" would permit. Tyndale, Matthew, Coverdale, the Great Bible, and the Genevan Bible were to be used where they agreed better with the text than the Bishops' Bible. The old ecclesiastical words were to be kept, for instance, reading "church" rather than "congregation." When a word had different meanings, the one most commonly used by the ancient fathers, agreeable to "the Propriety of the Place and the Analogy of the Faith," was to be used. Every man of a particular company was to take the same chapter or chapters, and after working by himself meet with the others to agree on the reading. When a company had finished a book, it was to be sent to the rest to be considered, and any differences were to be settled at a final general meeting of the chief persons of each company at the end of the work. Letters were to be sent from the bishops to the rest of the clergy, telling them of the translation in hand, and as many of them as were skillful in the languages and had "taken Pains in that kind" were to be exhorted to send in their observations to the company of translators concerned.

A final review of the translation was important, and twelve delegates from the six companies met together to review and revise the entire translation. The translators had before them other versions than those mentioned in the directions, including Luther's German translation, Zwingli's German translation, the Rheims and Douai Version, Olivétan's French translation, Latin translations by Pagninus, Münster, Castalio, and Erasmus, the Vulgate, Italian and Spanish translations, and the Plantin Polyglot. This list may not be particularly meaningful to the general reader, but it will suggest to him the care taken by the translators, who also used the Aramaic Targums, the Syriac New Testament, and the best Greek and Hebrew manuscripts then available. The completed translation included the Apocrypha.

An Authorized Version

Thus in 1611 was issued the King James Version. The title read: "The Holy Bible, Conteyning the Old Testament and the New: Newly Translated out of the Originall tongues & with the former translations diligently compared and reuised by his Maiesties speciall Commandement. Appointed to be read in Churches. Imprinted at London by Robert Barker, Printer to the Kings most Excellent Maiestie. Anno Dom. 1611." There is some question whether official action was taken justifying the statement "Appointed to be read in Churches," for there is no record to that effect. The churches referred to were those in the State Church.

It was an authorized version, although it is not the only authorized version. For this reason the designation of it as A.V. (Authorized Version) is less fortunate than the designation K.J.V. (King James Version), for the Great Bible of 1539 and the Bishops' Bible of 1568 were recognized officially for use in the churches, as we have seen, and were authorized versions. The English Revised Version of 1881–1885, which will be noted later, was inaugurated by the Convocation of Canterbury. We may also regard the Revised Standard Version as an authorized version, for its sponsor is the Division of Christian Education of the National Council of the Churches of Christ in the U.S.A., and the National Council itself, probably the largest Protestant Christian group ever to give official support to the making of an English version.

The Preface and Other Introductory Materials

The preface of the King James Version, "The Translators to the Reader," was written by one of the translators, Miles Smith, who was made bishop of Gloucester the year following the publication of the Bible. It is most unfortunate that modern printings of the King James Version do not include this preface, for it reveals some-

thing of the origin and purpose of the translation, the attitudes of
the translators, and contemporary reactions to the work of the translators. It would make it clear that the King James Version is not, as
many people think, the first translation ever made. It would suggest
the slowness and difficulties of the work, the aids used by the translators, and the great respect they had for the earlier translations. In
other words, reading this preface helps the reader of the Bible to
see the translation in truer perspective.

The preface begins with allusions to the criticisms being made of
the work, the kind of criticisms often made of new translations of
the Bible in any language, even though the new translation may be
a better one. The translators were realists, and knew the attitudes of
mind that the new translation would have to encounter. The preface
begins: "Zeale to promote the common good, whether it be by
deuising any thing our selues, or reuising that which hath bene
laboured by others, deserueth certainly much respect and esteeme,
but yet findeth but cold intertainment in the world . . . For, was
there euer any thing proiected, that sauoured any way of newnesse
or renewing, but the same endured many a storme of gaine-saying,
or opposition?" And after about one hundred lines of elaboration
and historical illustration of this theme, the preface writer then puts
his finger on the cause: "For he that medleth with mens Religion
in any part, medleth with their custome, nay, with their freehold;
and though they finde no content in that which they haue, yet they
cannot abide to heare of altering."

The importance of understanding the Scriptures by having them
in the vernacular is pointed out, with references to the Septuagint
and other Greek versions, the work of that great Biblical scholar
Origen (A.D. 186–253), the work of Jerome, the translations into
Arabic, Gothic, Anglo-Saxon, French, Syriac, the Rheims and
Douai translation, etc. A large section is devoted to answering
objections being made against the project, for "many mens mouths
haue been open a good while (and yet are not stopped) with
speeches about the Translation so long in hand, or rather perusals
of Translations made before: and aske what may be the reason,
what the necessitie of the employment: Hath the Church bene
deceiued, say they, all this while?" etc. The preface concludes with

a description of the purpose and nature of the work, the sources used, the problems of marginal notes and identity of phrasing. The use of Aramaic, Hebrew, Syriac, Greek, Latin, French, Italian, Spanish, and German translators or commentators is indicated, and the slow and scholarly character of the work, the translators not hesitating to " bring back to the anvil " that which they had already hammered.

Following the preface there was a calendar-almanac which gave the holy days and other data and the Scripture readings for morning and evening prayers. There was also a condensed almanac for thirty-nine years, a table "to finde Easter for euer," several tables for Scripture readings, a list of the holy days, and a table giving the names and order of the books of the Bible and the Apocrypha, with the number of chapters in each. Each chapter was headed by brief descriptions of the contents, as is often still done, with the running headnotes at the top of each column. The original engraved title page has Moses and Aaron in niches on either side of the title, beneath whom are seated Luke and John; Matthew and Mark appear in the upper panel, with Peter and James between them. The New Testament has its own engraved title page, with two Evangelists above and two below, and the shields of the twelve tribes on one side and of the twelve apostles on the other. Some bindings had among the introductory materials eighteen leaves of genealogies and a sheet containing a map of Canaan.

Revisions in the King James Version

We usually think of the King James Version as static and fixed, appearing now just as it appeared in 1611. But, like the earlier versions, the King James Version has gone through a series of revisions. An edition in 1613 had over 300 variations from the 1611 edition. Another revision appeared in 1629, and another in 1638. As a result of a bill brought before the Long Parliament in 1653 a revision committee was appointed in 1657, to make a revision if it should be found necessary, but the project was not undertaken. An extensive revision was published at Cambridge in 1762. There was another at Oxford in 1769, which included modernization of spelling, punctuation, correction of printing errors, etc., and in general this represents the version as it is known today. New marginal notes were added, and the chapter headings and running headnotes revised. To suggest some of the kinds of changes that have been made, we may place side by side a half dozen passages from the 1611 edition and from *The Westminster Study Edition of The Holy Bible* (The Westminster Press, 1948), the latter one of the finest of recent annotated Bibles using the King James Version.

Job 10:10:
1611: " Hast thou not powred me out as milke, and cruddled me like cheese? "
1948: " Hast thou not poured me out as milk, and curdled me like cheese? "

Jer. 26:23:
1611: " And they fet foorth Vrijah out of Egypt, and brought him vnto Iehoiakim the king, who slewe him with the sword, and cast his dead body into the graues of the common people."
1948: " And they fetched forth Urijah out of Egypt, and brought him unto Jehoiakim the king; who slew him with the sword, and cast his dead body into the graves of the common people."

Mark 10:18:
1611: " And Iesus said vnto him, Why callest thou me good? There is no man good, but one, *that is* God."
1948: " And Jesus said unto him, Why callest thou me good? *there* is none good but one, *that is,* God."

Acts 8:29:
1611: " Then the Spirit saide vnto Philip, Goe neere, and ioyne thy selfe to this charet."
1948: " Then the Spirit said unto Philip, Go near, and join thyself to this chariot."

Acts 28:8:
1611: " And it came to passe that the father of Publius lay sicke of a feuer, and of a bloody-flixe, to whom Paul entred in, and prayed,

and layed his hands on him, and healed him."

1948: "And it came to pass, that the father of Publius lay sick of a fever and of a bloody flux: to whom Paul entered in, and prayed, and laid his hands on him, and healed him."

Rom. 6:17:

1611: "But God bee thanked, that yee were the seruants of sinne: but ye haue obeyed from the heart that fourme of doctrine, which was deliuered you."

1948: "But God be thanked, that ye were the servants of sin, but ye have obeyed from the heart that form of doctrine which was delivered you."

We may point out that one change in Mark 10:18 was for obvious theological reasons, since the 1611 version implied the humanity of God.

PSALM 23 IN THE ORIGINAL KING JAMES VERSION

The reader may be interested in seeing the familiar Twenty-third Psalm as it appeared in the 1611 edition:

PSAL. XXIII
DAUIDS CONFIDENCE IN GODS GRACE
A Psalme of Dauid

The LORD *is* my shepheard, I shall not want.

2. He maketh me to lie downe in greene pastures: he leadeth mee beside the still waters.

3. He restoreth my soule: he leadeth me in the pathes of righteousness, for his names sake.

4. Yea, though I walke through the valley of the shadowe of death, I will feare no euill: for thou *art* with me, thy rod and thy staffe, they comfort me.

5. Thou preparest a table before me, in the presence of mine enemies: thou anointest my head with oyle, my cuppe runneth ouer.

6. Surely goodnes and mercie shall followe me all the daies of my life: and I will dwell in the house of the LORD for euer.

Some Literary Aspects of the King James Version

The English of the King James Version is often not, strictly speaking, the vernacular of the time when the translation was made. It is to a large extent the English of the preceding century, for there was incorporated in it a great deal of the phraseology of the sixteenth century translators, from Tyndale to the Bishops' Bible. As a result there are perhaps more words in the King James Version that have passed out of common usage than there would have been had it not been made with such dependence on the earlier translations. We shall later refer to the so-called archaisms, antiquated words and phrases, in the vocabulary of the King James Version. It is not surprising that some words in the King James Version are no longer current, or that their meaning has changed. There has been considerable illustration of changes within the English language in the quotations we have made in this volume. In a new translation today we would not want to keep words the meaning of which has been lost to current speech.

But with all the archaisms and despite the dependence of the King James Version on the earlier translations, we must not minimize the contribution made by the translators of the King James Version. If, as one author has estimated, sixty per cent of the text of the English Bible had reached its final form before the King James Version was produced, this still leaves no inconsiderable initiative to the 1611 translators. The translators not only drew upon the virtues and values of the previous versions, but they made many improvements in vocabulary, smoothness of flow of words, and aptness of translation. A simple but effective illustration of this is Matt. 11:28. Where the Bishops' Bible had read, " Come vnto me all ye that labour sore, and are laden, and I wyll ease you," the King James Version produced the much more happy phraseology, " Come vnto me all yee that labour, and are heauy laden, and I will giue you rest." The Revised Standard Version rightly keeps the King James Version rendering, with only the change necessary in line with its correction of the archaic " ye " and its use of the more simple preposition: " Come to me, all who labor and are heavy-laden, and I will give you rest."

Literary quality is a very difficult thing to estimate, as shown by the fact that one modern scholar comments that the obscurity of the King James Version is its outstanding trait, while another says that it is rare to catch the King James translators at a fault in their literary tact. For most people this is a fruitless debate. When a great hymn of the Church sings its way into our heart, we do not usually stop to examine its literary qualities. Some of the Bible is devotional and inspirational literature, and the test is the response it calls forth from the spirit and from the heart. This is not to minimize the extent to which the translator's primary concern should be the validity and accuracy of his translation, or the fact that there is much in the Scripture to which both mind and heart must respond.

An Example of Comparison

It is of interest to compare the 1611 edition of the King James Version with the Revised Standard Version of 1952. That the reader may see some of the differences, and also the strong indebtedness of the Revised Standard Version to the King James Version, we thus place side by side Isa. 43:15-21 in the two renderings:

K.J.V.:
(15) "I *am* the LORD, your Holy one, the Creatour of Israel, your King.
(16) Thus sayth the LORD, which maketh a way in the sea, and a path in the mightie waters:
(17) Which bringeth foorth the charet and horse, the armie and the power: they shall lie downe together, they shall not rise: they are extinct, they are quenched as towe.
(18) Remember yee not the former things, neither consider the things of olde.
(19) Behold, I will doe a new thing: now it shall spring foorth, shall yee not know it? I will euen make a way in the wildernesse, *and* riuers in the desert.
(20) The beast of the field shall honor mee, the dragons and the owles, because I giue waters in the wildernesse, *and* riuers in the desert, to giue drinke to my people, my chosen.

(21)   This people haue I formed for my selfe, they shall shew foorth my praise."

R.S.V.:

(15)   " ' I am the LORD, your Holy One,
           the Creator of Israel, your King.'
(16)   Thus says the LORD,
              who makes a way in the sea,
              a path in the mighty waters,
(17)   who brings forth chariot and horse,
              army and warrior;
           they lie down, they cannot rise,
              they are extinguished, quenched like a wick:
(18)   ' Remember not the former things,
              nor consider the things of old.
(19)   Behold, I am doing a new thing;
              now it springs forth, do you not perceive it?
           I will make a way in the wilderness
              and rivers in the desert.
(20)   The wild beasts will honor me,
              the jackals and the ostriches;
           for I give water in the wilderness,
              rivers in the desert,
           to give drink to my chosen people,
              the people whom I formed for myself
              that they might declare my praise.' "

The Revised Standard Version in its representation of the poetic form of this passage, in its avoidance of archaisms, and in the accuracy of its translation marks a notable advance, while at the same time it preserves the best in the King James Version, for its indebtedness to the King James Version is obvious.

V ✦

TO THE AMERICAN STANDARD VERSION

THE King James Version represents the culmination or highest point of English Bible translation up to the seventeenth century. It seems almost as though the translations of the earlier centuries had been moving toward this great climax. They were the preparation and it was the fulfillment. They conspired to give substance to a work that would stand the test of the needs of the Church and of individuals for more than three centuries. When in 1881–1885 and in 1901 it was to be revised as the English Revised Version and the American Standard Version, it was to be essentially the scholars rather than the people and the Church who were calling for a revision. Not until our own day has there been what we may call a more general sentiment that the King James Version should be revised, and this for reasons that will be evident in our next chapter.

There have been many translations of the Bible since the King James Version was issued in 1611. Some of them were by individuals and some of them by groups of scholars who recognized the need of correcting the King James Version. Some have been authorized or approved by ecclesiastical bodies. The development of Biblical scholarship, the discoveries of more ancient manuscripts, and the increased knowledge of the languages involved have been part of the motivation. It is easier for us to appreciate the advances that have been made in the sciences, especially in physics and in medicine, than it is for us to appreciate the progress in Biblical scholarship. The evidences for the developments in atomic research and in the "wonder drugs" are dramatic. But there has been a comparable progress made in Biblical researches.

Some of the translations that we shall describe are attempts to put the Bible into the contemporary language, deliberately avoiding the expressions and phraseology of the King James Version. It will not be denied that there are values in such " fresh " translations. But it is also true that it is possible to make a translation of the Bible in up-to-date English which is at the same time " in the tradition," and which preserves the cadence and beauty and much of the phraseology of the King James Version. Such a translation should be acceptable for church use as well as for home and personal use.

It is important that a translation exist that is acceptable for both church and private use. Some of the fresh translations are helpful for personal use without at the same time finding wide usage in the churches. As long as the Church is historically minded, as it should be, and is conscious of its debt to the past and its role in human history, it will find inadequate a completely " modernized " translation. But on the other hand, the church cannot use in its services a version that does not have an appeal to the modern man. The church and home must be integrated in the religious life. Our religious educators of today believe that everything possible should be done to make the church at home in the home, and the home at home in the church. Bible translations, like religion itself, should not be merely a Sunday affair. The King James Version is today used in both home and church. But can a translation be made that will be sufficiently " in the tradition " to preserve those historic values which are so important for organized Christianity, and which will at the same time be in good, dignified, readable, contemporary English? Such a translation might find greater personal use than the older versions. Perhaps it is toward such a translation that events in the history of translation have been moving in the last two or three centuries.

MANUSCRIPTS OF THE HEBREW OLD TESTAMENT

This is not the place to discuss in detail the complicated problems of Biblical manuscripts and their importance. But we cannot entirely ignore this matter. There exist today no manuscripts of the Old or the New Testament in the handwriting of its authors. " Original " copies of the Bible do not exist. The Bible was not all written at one time, so that in any case one could hardly speak of a "first edition" of the Bible. One of the problems of the Biblical scholar is the recovery and evaluation of Biblical manuscripts. Up until the recent discoveries to be mentioned in the next chapter, there existed no very early Hebrew manuscripts of the Old Testament. A manuscript of the Latter Prophets (Isaiah, Jeremiah, Ezekiel, and the Twelve Minor Prophets) in Leningrad, Russia, is dated to A.D. 916. A manuscript of the Pentateuch in the British Museum in London belongs to the ninth century A.D. A manuscript of the Former Prophets (Joshua, Judges, Samuel, Kings) and Latter Prophets in the Karaite synagogue in Cairo, Egypt, is dated to A.D. 895. A copy of the complete Old Testament in the synagogue of the Sephardic Jews in Aleppo, Syria, belongs to the tenth century A.D. This is the oldest existing manuscript of the whole Old Testament in Hebrew. There are known fragments of the Hebrew Bible that go back possibly as early as the sixth century A.D. Up until recently, the earliest known portion of the Old Testament in Hebrew was the so-called Nash Papyrus, which came from Egypt and contained the Ten Commandments and Deut. 6:4; it belongs possibly to the second century B.C.

Three Early Greek Manuscripts

Although the earliest known copies of any considerable portion of the Old Testament in Hebrew have thus come from as late as the ninth and tenth centuries A.D., there are in existence earlier copies of the complete or nearly complete Old Testament in translation. We will mention here by way of illustration three early manuscripts of the Septuagint or Greek translation, which are very important for trying to recover the earlier form of the Hebrew text of the Old Testament. When used with caution, they may give some indication of the character of the Hebrew text of which the Septuagint is a translation. One of these early Septuagint manuscripts is the Codex Alexandrinus, given this name because it had originally come from Alexandria in Egypt. In 1624, thirteen years after the publication of the King James Version, it was given by the patriarch of Constantinople for presentation to King James I. Because of James's death, the presentation was actually made to his successor, Charles I.

The manuscript was written in the fifth century A.D. It is now in the British Museum.

The second of these manuscripts is the Codex Vaticanus. It is the most important of the manuscripts of the Greek Bible, and was written in the fourth century. It has been in the Vatican library at Rome since before 1481, and was first made known in 1533, but it was not then published. Napoleon carried the manuscript to Paris as a prize of war, where it remained until 1815, when it was returned to Rome. It was studied while at Paris, and its importance first made known in 1810. Inadequate editions of it were published in 1857 and 1859, and a more perfect edition of it was published by the famous German scholar, Constantin von Tischendorf, in 1867. Complete photographs of it were made available in 1889-1890.

The third manuscript is the Codex Sinaiticus, given this name because it was discovered at the Monastery of St. Catherine at Mt. Sinai. The story of this manuscript is particularly interesting. In 1844, Tischendorf recovered forty-three leaves of the manuscript from a basket at the monastery. Apparently he saved them from being burned as wastepaper. Later, in 1859, when he was revisiting the monastery, he was shown a manuscript of loose leaves which proved to be the same manuscript from which the forty-three leaves had come, and which contained 199 more leaves of the Old Testament, and also the entire New Testament, as well as two Apocryphal books of the New Testament, the Epistle of Barnabas and the Shepherd of Hermas. Tischendorf reports the "transport of joy" he felt at such a find. The forty-three leaves are now at Leipzig. The rest of the manuscript was presented to the czar of Russia and was put in the Imperial Library at St. Petersburg (now Leningrad). In 1933 the Russian Government, needing the money, sold it to the British Museum for 100,000 pounds, which at the predepression rates would be the equivalent of $500,000. The manuscript was written in the fourth century A.D. None of these three important manuscripts, the Codex Alexandrinus, the Codex Vaticanus, or the Codex Sinaiticus, was available to the translators of the King James Version.

Toward a Better Greek Text of the New Testament

The King James Version of the New Testament had been based mainly on Beza's Greek text, which had been printed in 1598. Professor Craig writes, " Though he had available what we know to be much better manuscripts, Beza had followed the text of Erasmus, which was based on late and corrupt medieval manuscripts." (*An Introduction to the Revised Standard Version of the New Testament,* p. 15.) The first edition of what was to be regarded as "the received text" (Textus Receptus) was published in 1624, based on a text published by Stephanus (1546 ff.) and Beza, and the second edition claimed optimistically that there was in it nothing *immutatum aut corruptum* (changed or corrupted).

It was thought by some that the Greek text of the New Testament as known was unalterable and certain. But since the time of the King James Version a great deal of work has been done on the New Testament Greek text. The recovery of the Codex Alexandrinus inspired such study, and ancient manuscripts were compared and their variations noted. The eighteenth century saw much advance. So, for instance, John Mill in 1707 published a new folio edition of the Greek New Testament (Stephanus' text), and cited more than 30,000 variant readings. The New Testament published in 1751–1752 by Wetstein quoted readings from more than three hundred manuscripts. In the nineteenth century Carolus Lachmann of Berlin showed the inadequacy of the " received text " by publishing in 1831 a revised Greek New Testament in which he tried to establish a fourth century text. Tischendorf issued eight editions of the Greek New Testament, the last published in 1869–1872.

It was, however, two Cambridge scholars, Professors B. F. Westcott and F. J. A. Hort, who contributed most to textual criticism of the New Testament in the nineteenth century with their analysis and classification of Greek New Testament manuscripts, trying to establish the most nearly original text. In 1881, within a week of the publication of the English Revised Version, Westcott and Hort published their " New Testament in the Original Greek." This was the text used by the translators, which varied from the " received text " in nearly six thousand instances. The changes were made necessary by the discovery and analysis of many early manuscripts. Although we do not today have a perfect Greek text from which to translate, even as we have no such Hebrew text, since 1611 great progress has been made in determining the older and more valid readings of the Greek manuscripts, and today it is possible to go far beyond Westcott and Hort. Both Westcott and Hort were on the committee that produced the English Revised Version of the New Testament in 1881.

Some Eighteenth and Nineteenth Century Translations

Before we come to the discussion of the English Revised Version we should note briefly a few of the many attempts to translate the Bible into English between the time of the King James Version and the English Revised Version. Few people realize that among the translators of the Bible are such persons as John Wesley and Noah Webster. The following discussion is concerned largely with translations not " in the tradition."

The first we shall mention is the translation by William Mace, a Presbyterian minister. In 1729 he published " The New Testament in Greek and English. Containing the Original Text Corrected from the Authority of the most Authentic Manuscripts: and a New Version Form'd agreeably to the Illustrations of the most Learned Commentators and Critics: with Notes and Verious Readings, and a Copious Alphabetical Index." He made corrections of the " received text " on the basis of early manuscripts. In his translations he broke sharply with the traditional renderings, and at times his translation amounted to a paraphrase. So in I Cor. 13:4 he read, " Social affection is patient, is kind," and in I Cor. 14:1, " Cultivate social virtue." Matt. 19:24 read, " It is easier for a cable to go through the eye of a needle, than for a rich man to enter the divine kingdom."

John Wesley in 1755 published a translation of the New Testament, with notes to " assist the unlearned reader." He wrote in the preface: " I am the rather induced to do what little I can in this way, because I can do nothing else; being prevented by my present weakness from either traveling or preaching. But, blessed be God, I can still read, and write, and think. O that it may be to his glory! "

He appreciated the need of a translation that could be understood by the people, for he continued: " I write chiefly for plain, unlettered men, who understand only their mother tongue, and yet reverence and love the word of God, and have a desire to save their souls." It was a good translation, a revision of the King James Version where he felt it necessary for better understanding. The arrangement in sense paragraphs was one of its important features. He read I Cor. 13:4, " Love suffereth long, and is kind," and v. 13, " And now abide these three, faith, hope, love; but the greatest of these is love." John Wesley in his preface describes " the common English translation," that is, the King James Version, as being " in general, so far as I can judge, abundantly the best that I have seen." And he continues: " Yet I do not say that it is incapable of being brought, in several places, nearer to the original. Neither will I affirm that the Greek copies from which this translation was made are always the most correct; and therefore I shall take the liberty, as occasion may require, to make here and there a small alteration." The Wesley New Testament with its notes is still printed today and sees considerable use.

A " New and Literal Translation " of the Bible by Anthony Purver, a Quaker, appeared in 1764. Its break with the tradition may be illustrated by S. of Sol. 2:12, where " The flowers appear on the earth " becomes " Earth's lap displays her infant flowers," and by the Lord's Prayer, where " hallowed " becomes " sacredly reverenced." In 1768, Edward Harwood published " A Liberal Translation of the New Testament," patterned after the current manner of translating the Greek classics, a " liberal and diffusive " translation, designed to appeal to men of cultivated and improved minds, especially youth. It was a very free translation or paraphrase, in which, for instance, the Lord's Prayer is about six times the length in the more traditional versions. Harwood has been called the " Beau Brummell " among translators. Gilbert Wakefield in 1791 issued a Unitarian version. Alexander Campbell, in 1826, in an edition of " The Sacred Writings and the Apostles and Evangelists of Jesus Christ Commonly Called the New Testament Translated from the Original Greek by George Campbell, James Macknight, and Philip Doddridge, Doctors of the Church of Scotland," published by him in Virginia, wrote in the preface: "It is probable that a new translation into our language will never again be undertaken by public authority. The People would not now submit to any that would be imposed on them by such authority, and they will not agree among themselves to select persons in whose judgment and fidelity they might repose confidence."

Rodolphus Dickinson published at Boston in 1833 "A New and Corrected Version of the New Testament," being caustically critical of the literary quality of the King James Version. Noah Webster's revised version of the Bible was published in 1833, and was "in the Common Version, with Amendments of the Language." In view of his work on the English dictionary and his interest in the English language, he was naturally much concerned with the changes that had occurred in the English language since 1611 and in questions of English grammar. He corrected, for instance, the ungrammatical " Whom do men say that I the son of man am? " in Matt. 16:13, to " Who do men say," etc., a correction followed by the later authorized versions. He wrote in the preface to his translation: " In my own view of this subject, a version of the Scriptures for popular use should consist of words expressing the sense which is most common, in popular usage, so that the first ideas suggested should be the true meaning of such words, according to the original languages. That many words in the present version fail to do this is certain."

One of the curiosities in the history of the English Bible is the translation of the Bible made by Julia E. Smith in 1876, from the Hebrew and Greek, using the same English word for the same Hebrew or Greek word everywhere. She thought that this gave " much clearer understanding of the text." The end result, however, was much nonsense and a lot of obscurity and almost complete mistranslation. She translated the verbs in the future tense in the historical narratives, giving the reader the impression that everything in those narratives, including the acts of creation in Gen., ch. 1, was yet to happen. The extent of the obscurity is suggested by Jer. 22:23, presented as a complete sentence and reading, " Thou dwelling in Lebanon, building a nest in the cedars, how being compassionated in pangs coming to thee the pain as of her bringing forth." A recent history of the English Bible rashly speaks of her as

a woman of scholarly attainments. She illustrates dramatically a
fact that some people do not appreciate, namely, that a word has
more than one meaning, and in translation the more specific meaning of a word in a particular context has to be determined from
that context.

THE ENGLISH REVISED VERSION, 1881–1885

There were numerous demands for revision of the King James
Version in the nineteenth century. Some people found it necessary
to publish vindications of the King James Version in the light of
such demands. In the Lower House of Convocation in 1856 the
question of revision was introduced, but it did not then find sufficient support. As is hinted in our earlier discussion, the recovery
of a more accurate Greek text of the New Testament was probably
the most influential factor among those influences which brought
about the production of a new authorized version, the English
Revised Version of 1881–1885. The first motion as it was made in the
Upper House of the Convocation of Canterbury on February 10,
1870, was that a committee from both the Upper House and the
Lower House should be appointed to report on the desirability of
revising the King James Version of the New Testament. An amend-
ment to the motion included the Old Testament.

The initiative for the translation thus came through the Church
of England, although the fifty-four members of the Revision Committee included the Baptist, Congregationalist, Methodist, Presbyterian, and Unitarian denominations. There had been some attempt
to keep the translation within the hands of the Church of England,
but this failed. The largest single group represented was the Church
of England, but it was nevertheless a real interdenominational
group of translators. There was at first a strong reaction by some
over the appointment on the New Testament company of G. V.
Smith, a Unitarian. Among the translators were such men of great
scholarship and ability as Ginsburg, Davidson, Driver, Sayce,
Wright, Hort, Westcott, Eadie, and others. The revisers worked
without financial payment other than their expenses, which were
paid by an arrangement with the University Presses of Oxford and
Cambridge on considerations of exclusive right of publication within

Her Majesty's kingdom. The translators were divided into two companies, one on the Old Testament and one on the New Testament, with twenty-seven in each.

The general principles laid down for the guidance of the translators included the following: They were to make as few alterations as possible in the text of the King James Version and to limit the expression of such alterations to the language of the King James and earlier versions. They were to use as the text from which to translate "that for which the evidence is decidedly preponderating." They were to revise the italics, paragraphs, and punctuation, and also the headings of chapters and pages. In the completed translation the headings of chapters and pages were actually omitted. Each company was to go twice over the portion revised, and the first time a simple majority decided the reading, but the second time a two-thirds vote was necessary to make a change. Especially important was the abandonment of the old division of the books into chapters and verses in favor of arrangement in paragraphs, although the chapter and verse numbers were retained for convenience of reference. This is now more or less standard procedure in Bible translations, and the Westminster Study Edition uses this arrangement in its presentation of the King James Version. In the poetic books an arrangement of lines to indicate the parallelism characteristic of Hebrew poetry was followed, but it is unfortunate that the reviewers felt that this should not be extended to the "prophetical books," which they considered "lofty impassioned prose."

The translators in the "Revisers' Preface" state that it was not their duty to make a new translation, but to revise one already existing, and they indicate that they departed from the King James Version only when they disagreed with the meaning as translated in 1611, or where it was necessary to make uniform the translation of parallel passages where the Hebrew was identical, or where archaic or obscure words had to be made clear, or where the reading of an earlier version seemed preferable, or where a slight change would bring out the meaning. It is also affirmed that as regards the language of the King James Version, the revisers "thought it no part of their duty to reduce it to conformity with modern usage, and have therefore left untouched all archaisms, whether of language or construction, which though not in familiar use cause a reader no embarrassment and lead to no misunderstanding." As H. W. Robinson says, the revisers aimed at being both Elizabethan and intelligible. Had the translators followed a different policy at this point, the translation might have attained more permanent popularity than it did. It was also a translation that was as literal as it could be without being impossible English, and as a result is much more stilted than the smooth-flowing English of the King James Version. Because of this the English Revised Version is more useful than the King James Version to the student of Hebrew who wants the help of a literal translation, and it is easier to prepare an accurate concordance of it; but such is not the primary purpose of a Bible translation. Nor is it the best way to learn Hebrew!

The New Testament company worked for ten and a half years, finishing in November, 1880, the publication taking place the following year. The Old Testament company worked for fourteen years, completing work in 1884, the complete Bible thus being published in 1885. Co-operating with the English revisers was an American committee, divided into Old Testament and New Testament companies. The English revisers sent copies of their work to the American committee, and promised to take into special consideration all the American suggestions, and to allow the American revisers to present in an appendix all the remaining differences of reading and rendering of importance rejected by the English committee. The American revisers agreed not to issue an edition of their own for fourteen years. The American committee by agreement bore its own expenses, raised at first by voluntary contributions, and then by offering memorial volumes of the New Testament or the Old Testament to those contributing certain amounts.

Among the suggestions of the American revisers rejected by the English committee was the use of " Jehovah " for " LORD " or " GOD," and the avoidance of archaisms by using " patched " instead of " clouted," " cakes " instead of " cracknels," " attired " instead of " tired," " fined " instead of " amerced," " settings " instead of " ouches," " astonished " instead of " astonied," " be hurtful to " instead of " endamage," " turned away from " instead of " eschewed," " hump " instead of " bunches " (of a camel), " betray " instead of "bewray," "capital" instead of "chapiter," "report" instead of "bruit," "lewd" instead of "whorish," etc. The preface by the English revisers notes that in retaining archaisms of language and construction "they will disappoint the large English-speaking race on the other side of the Atlantic," but that they were "prepared to agree to a friendly difference of opinion."

The initial reception of the English Revised Version was beyond expectation. A telegram sent from London to America four days after the New Testament was issued on May 17, 1881, reported the sale of two million copies in London alone, and within less than a year three million copies in all had been sold. The Chicago *Tribune* and the Chicago *Times* reprinted the New Testament in its entirety on May 22 in their papers. It is said that the *Tribune* employed for the purpose ninety-two compositors and five correctors, and the whole book was completed in twelve hours. A historian of the English Bible, writing eleven years after the publication of the English Revised Version, affirmed his belief that this new version was "a finality for years to come." The Convocation of Canterbury in 1899 voted in favor of the use of the English Revised Version in public worship in the Church of England where the clergy and people so desired. But this translation, like others, met with strong opposition in some quarters; its use in public worship was deplored; it was criticized for its stilted, pedantic English; objection was taken to the changes made on the basis of the versions; and the theological implications of some of its changes were criticized.

The American Standard Version, 1901

The need for the American committee to publish a version containing their suggestions became apparent, especially since in 1881–1883 two unauthorized editions of the New Testament were published in this country by incorporating the readings suggested by the American committee which were put in the Appendix of the English Revised Version. The Oxford and Cambridge University Presses printed a similar edition in 1898. In contrast with the English committee, the American committee had continued in existence. On August 26, 1901, the American revisers issued "The Holy Bible, containing the Old and New Testaments translated out of the original tongues, being the version set forth A.D. 1611 compared with the most ancient authorities and revised A.D. 1881–1885. Newly Edited by the American Revision Committee A.D. 1901. Standard Edition." The publishers, Thomas Nelson & Sons, held the copyright "to insure purity of text," i.e., in order to provide a protection against such unauthorized editions as the three just mentioned.

This American Standard Version, as it has come to be known, was much more than a transference of readings from the Appendix of the English Revised Version. As the translators say in the Preface, the Appendix itself was in need of revision due to the circumstances under which it had been prepared, which had involved considerable haste. Besides, it had contained only a selected number of the American committee's suggestions. The American Standard Version substituted "Jehovah" for "Lord" and "God," as they had suggested in the Appendix. They felt they were restoring "this personal name, with its wealth of sacred associations . . . to the place in the sacred text to which it has an unquestionable claim." We may question the wisdom of this change, as we shall see in our discussion of the Revised Standard Version.

But there is little question of the superiority of the American Standard Version. In some instances it was thought that the English Revised Version had needlessly departed from the King James Version. The American Standard Version contained a greater consistency of translation where the Hebrew or Greek word had the same meaning. There were a number of changes for the sake of euphemism, and there was greater consistency in using "its" rather than "his" when the antecedent was neuter. More particularly, certain archaisms of vocabulary and diction were not kept, although one now feels that the revisers did not go far enough in this respect. Certain "bad and outlandish" Hebraisms were abolished, although here also the translators might have been more thorough. Considerable improvement was made in marginal notes and paragraphing. Headings to the pages indicated the general content of the page. With a few notable exceptions, historians of the English Bible have not always given the American Standard Version the credit it deserves as an important step in the progress of Bible translation. Yet it is in a real sense not a separate version so much as an

American edition of the Revised Version.

Despite the initial success of the English Revised Version, the American Standard Version has been more popular in this country than the English Revised Version in England. But, as one scholar has phrased it, both the English Revised Version and the American Standard Version were undertaken prematurely. The discoveries of the first half of the twentieth century have been so revolutionary that they have demanded a new translation that incorporates the fruits of our newer knowledge. It is now possible to make a much more accurate translation than could have been made in 1881–1885 or 1901. A brief account of the new discoveries that have relevance to the translation of the Bible will be our concern in the following chapter.

VI ✍

NEW LIGHT ON THE BIBLE: A HALF CENTURY OF DISCOVERY

Excavation Assists Translation

B OTH through archaeological research and through the recovery and study of ancient manuscripts, notable progress has been made in our understanding of the Bible since the beginning of this century. The period between the two world wars saw intensive archaeological activity in Palestine, and something of the fruits of such research may be seen in W. F. Albright's *The Archaeology of Palestine* (Pelican Books, 1949); Millar Burrows' *What Mean These Stones?* (American Schools of Oriental Research, 1941); and C. C. McCown's *The Ladder of Progress in Palestine* (Harper & Brothers, 1943). The inscriptional material thus discovered offers assistance to the translator, and his understanding of the material cultures of ancient Palestine as revealed by the archaeological researches may also provide help. The arrangements of cities, with their streets, gates, towers, water systems, etc., are better understood, and the meaning of the Biblical text is sometimes clarified. For instance, the King James Version translates the Hebrew word *rehob* as " street," and in Esth. 4:6 refers to the " street of the city, which was before the king's gate," or in II Chron. 32:6 to the people gathered " in the street of the gate of the city," etc. But both the root meaning of the word and the excavations make it clear that what is meant is the open space or square, the market place, before the city gate, and so the Revised Standard Version translates II Chron. 32:6, " In the square at the gate of the city."

The various forms of pottery or dishes used by the people in Biblical days are known to us through the excavations, and some association with the Hebrew vocabulary is possible, as Professor James L. Kelso has shown in his book, *The Ceramic Vocabulary of the Old Testament* (New Haven, 1948). Where the King James Version reads " candlestick " for the Hebrew *menorah* in the Old Testament, or " candle " or " candlestick " for the Greek *luchnia* in the New Testament, the Revised Standard Version reads " lampstand " or " lamp "; it is now known that candles were unknown in Biblical days, and the kind of lampstands and lamps used may be illustrated from archaeological materials.

Archaeological specimens of a type of hand censer make it probable that the Hebrew word *kaph,* translated in the King James Version as " spoon " (see Ex. 25:29; 37:16; Num. 4:7; etc.) is probably a censer, and the Revised Standard Version renders the word " dish for incense." In the King James and English Revised Versions *hammanim* is translated " images," and it is translated "sun-images " in the American Standard Version (see Lev. 26:30; Isa. 17:8; 27:9; Ezek. 6:4; etc.), but neither is correct. The reference is to incense altars, as is evidenced by an altar of incense from Palmyra, which has this word inscribed on it, and this fits the contexts and explains the reading in the Revised Standard Version. It is now known that the word that is usually translated " sapphire " does not refer to the kind of stone we designate by that name, but rather it refers to a blue stone called " lapis lazuli "; seals, beads, jewels, and inlays made from this stone appear in the excavations, and the Revised Standard Version margin so identifies it. These are but a few of many examples that could be given.

INSCRIPTIONAL AIDS TO TRANSLATION

The inscriptional material recovered by the archaeologists has also provided important helps. The Hebrew vocabulary is better understood because of the mass of materials for comparison made available from the ancient cognate (related) languages such as Aramaic and Akkadian (Assyrian and Babylonian). A considerable amount of Canaanite inscriptional material is now known. This is important since we may class the Canaanite and Hebrew languages together; the Old Testament designates Hebrew as " the language of Canaan " in Isa. 19:18. The most significant " Canaanite " inscriptions come from a temple library in the north Canaanite territory at modern Ras Shamra, ancient Ugarit, near the coast southwest of Antioch. The library, lying between the temple of Baal and the temple of Dagon, contained hundreds of inscriptions written on clay tablets in an alphabetic cuneiform (wedge-shaped) script. The library was discovered in the excavations at Ugarit in 1929, and it may be dated to the early fourteenth century B.C., which, according to some scholars, would be about the time the Hebrews under Joshua were entering the Promised Land. The inscriptions consist largely of myths of the gods and goddesses of the Canaanites.

A glossary or dictionary of these inscriptions published in 1947 by Cyrus Gordon contains 2,309 words. As a result of the discovery of these tablets, many a Biblical passage has been made clearer through the light they throw on the Hebrew vocabulary. A goodly number of Hebrew words occur only once in the Old Testament, and their meaning is not always known. It is also to be expected that the Hebrew literature would contain many Canaanite forms of diction and imagery, and some of the Hebrew words may be classified as Canaanite archaisms. The poetry forms of the Canaanites and Hebrews naturally have much in common.

We may give a few examples of the aid given to the translators by these inscriptions from Ugarit. In Ps. 68:4 the description of God as "him that rideth through the desert " (English Revised and American Standard Versions) is to be read without emendation (i.e., change of the Hebrew text) with the Revised Standard Version as "him who rides upon the clouds," paralleling the description of Baal in these tablets as "the rider on the clouds." It is with the help of the Ugaritic texts that the Revised Standard Version reconstructs and makes intelligible the first line of Prov. 26:23, reading the verse,

> "Like the glaze covering an earthen vessel
> are smooth lips with an evil heart."

Compare the King James Version:

"Burning lips and a wicked heart are like a potsherd covered with silver dross."

In Ezek. 43:7, 9 we should probably interpret the meaning of a word as it appears in the Ugaritic texts and read " monuments of their kings " (see Revised Standard Version margin), rather than " dead bodies of their kings " ; see also Lev. 26:30 where " monuments of your idols " gives more understandable meaning than " carcases of your idols." In the light of a Ugaritic parallel, the original form of the second line of II Sam. 1:21 from David's lament may have read:

" Let there be no dew or rain upon you, nor upsurging of the deep! "

Contrast the " fields of offerings " in the King James Version. Professor Albright has shown the importance of these texts particularly for understanding the poetry in the Old Testament, such as the oracles of Balaam in Num., chs. 23; 24, the blessing of Moses in Deut., ch. 33, the psalm of Habakkuk in Hab., ch. 3, and in certain of the psalms. The texts support the traditional rendering " moved " in Gen. 1:2, rather than the often suggested " was brooding upon " (English Revised and American Standard Version margin).

We will list briefly some of the other inscriptions provided through archaeological research. From about the same time as the Ugaritic tablets there are the Amarna Letters, clay tablets written in Akkadian cuneiform by the rulers of Palestine and Syria to the Egyptian Pharaohs Amenhotep III and Akhnaton. Still earlier, from the eighteenth century B.C., come over 20,000 tablets discovered in 1936–1939 at Mari on the Euphrates, and the language is, in Albright's opinion, virtually identical with the ancestral Hebrew of the Patriarchs. There is an important Phoenician royal inscription from Karatepe in Cilicia, belonging to the ninth or eighth century B.C., discovered in 1946. There are Aramaic inscriptions from Syria from between 900 and 600 B.C.

The inscriptional material from Palestine itself is important though not extensive. Most familiar is the famous Moabite Stone, written by Mesha, king of Moab (see II Kings 3:4), first known in 1868, and the Siloam inscription inscribed by Hezekiah on the tunnel of the water system mentioned in II Kings 20:20, found in 1880. There are also some seventy ostraca (inscriptions on pottery shards) disclosed by the excavations at Samaria in 1908–1910, dated perhaps to the reign of Jeroboam II; they are lists or receipts of wine and oil. Of great importance are the ostraca from Lachish, discovered in 1935 and 1938, which are largely letters written by a Judean military leader to the Judean military governor of Lachish in 589 b.c., when Nebuchadnezzar was attacking Judah preparatory to his attack on Jerusalem. They thus belong to the time of the prophet Jeremiah and King Zedekiah. There are twenty-one of these ostraca, of which a half dozen are legible. We may also mention an eleventh to tenth century b.c. calendar from Gezer.

Coming from a Jewish colony at Elephantine in Egypt are fifth century b.c. Aramaic papyri, discovered in 1903. More of these papyri have just recently come to light. They reflect many phases of the life of this community. It will be recalled that this is the century of Ezra, and that The Book of Ezra is written partly in Aramaic, as is also a large section of The Book of Daniel.

THE DEAD SEA SCROLLS

A most spectacular discovery of recent date has to do with manuscripts. During the spring or summer of 1947 a Bedouin in search of a lost goat discovered a cave in the Wilderness of Judea near Ain Fashkha, at the northeast shore of the Dead Sea. From the cave he and a fellow Arab took a number of ancient manuscripts which they found there. Four of these were eventually bought by the metropolitan or archbishop of St. Mark's Syrian Orthodox Monastery in Jerusalem. In February of 1948 they were shown to Dr. John Trever, who was then acting director of the American School of Oriental Research in Jerusalem. Upon examination he recognized that one of them was a scroll of The Book of Isaiah. By comparing the script or form of the letters with the Nash Papyrus (see p. 63), he reached the conclusion that it belonged to the second century b.c. It would thus be about a thousand years earlier than the otherwise earliest known copy of The Book of Isaiah in Hebrew!

Further examination disclosed the remaining three scrolls to be a "commentary" on Habakkuk, a Manual of Discipline, and the apocryphal Book of Lamech. The last of these is in particularly poor condition, and has not yet been unrolled. The recovery of this lost apocryphal book, known to us from a reference to it in a Greek list of apocryphal books, is of special importance. It is written in Aramaic, and the other three scrolls are in Hebrew. A number of scrolls that had come from the cave were secured by Professor Sukenik, of the Hebrew University at Jerusalem. Among these is a collection of thanksgiving hymns, a scroll called " The War of the Children of Light Against the Children of Darkness," and a scroll containing Isa., chs. 48 to 59. In contrast with the complete scroll of Isaiah, this copy had a spelling much closer to that of the standard or Masoretic Text.

The cave in which the manuscripts had been found was excavated in the first half of 1949. From it were recovered hundreds of pieces of inscribed parchment, varying in size from small fragments to a third of a scroll. Some inscribed fragments of papyrus were found. There was also considerable linen around, in which the scrolls had been wrapped. Many pieces of pottery were recovered, belonging to the jars that had contained the scrolls and to bowls that had been used as covers for the jars. The pottery was pre-Roman in date, and it is estimated that there had been at least 40 jars and perhaps more than 200 manuscripts in the cave. The jars give support to the early date given to the manuscripts. Some fragments of a Roman pot and a spout of a Roman lamp suggest the cave had been entered in Roman times, perhaps as far back as the time of Origen, as noted on p. 82.

Many scholars examining the style of writing of the scrolls believe that the scrolls may not be all of the same date, but should all be placed in the second century and the early first century B.C. Not all scholars have been convinced of this early date, but the evidence seems to favor it. The new carbon radioactivity test tried on some of the linen from the cave produced results consistent with this date. The scroll of Isaiah may be among the earlier manuscripts in the cave. The manuscripts may have been put in the cave by the sect whose Manual of Discipline was found among them. The sect seems to have affinities with the Covenanters of Damascus, the Essenes, and perhaps even the John the Baptist movement, as Professor W. H. Brownlee has suggested.

Among the manuscript bits from the cave are several small fragments of the book of Leviticus in an earlier script, which have been dated to before 400 B.C. by at least one scholar, but not far from 100 B.C. by others. There were also recovered fragments of Genesis, Deuteronomy, Judges, and the Book of Jubilees. Among the manuscript fragments brought to this country with the four scrolls by Archbishop Samuel, of St. Mark's Monastery, are three fragments of Daniel, and they may belong not far from the time of the composition of The Book of Daniel around 165 B.C. It may be that other manuscripts and fragments from the cave will turn up. The Palestine Archaeological Museum has acquired fragments of manuscripts that include some belonging to the scroll of the Book of Lamech. There are also five short fragments that belong to the Isaiah scroll that Hebrew University had acquired, and some extensive fragments that belong to the Manual of Discipline.

The archbishop gave the American Schools of Oriental Research permission to publish the four Dead Sea Scrolls in his possession.[1] The effect of the discovery of the Isaiah scroll has been to give us increased confidence in the Hebrew text as it had been preserved for us. Despite differences in spelling and grammatical forms, it is essentially the book as preserved in the Masoretic Text. The Revised Standard Version translators of the Old Testament naturally considered this ancient manuscript while working on The Book of Isaiah. They followed in fourteen places the differences it presented. None of these was of extreme importance, and they were sometimes supported by the versions. For instance, in Isa. 14:30 the Revised Standard Version reads,

> "But I will kill your root with famine,
> and your remnant I will slay."

[1] The following have been published: *The Dead Sea Scrolls of St. Mark's Monastery,* Vol. I, *The Isaiah Manuscript and the Habakkuk Commentary,* 1950; Vol. II, *Fascicle 2, Plates and Transcription of the Manual of Discipline,* 1951, edited by Millar Burrows with the assistance of John C. Trever and William H. Brownlee, published by the American Schools of Oriental Research, New Haven. *The Dead Sea Manual of Discipline,* Translation and Notes, by William H. Brownlee, Supplementary Studies Nos. 10–12, *Bulletin of the American Schools of Oriental Research,* 1951.

This is with the Isaiah scroll and the Vulgate, the received Hebrew text reading, " He will slay," and so the King James Version. There is little question that in Isa. 15:9 we should read (at two points) with the Isaiah scroll and the Vulgate " Dibon " (the well-known city of the Moabites), instead of " Dimon."

The discovery of the cave and its scrolls may in reality be a rediscovery. A history of Jewish sects written about A.D. 937 tells of a sect called the Magharites (cf. Arabic *maghar,* " cave ") because their books were found in a cave. In a letter written by a Nestorian patriarch of Seleucia, Timothy I, about A.D. 800, it is said that some Jewish converts related how an Arab followed his dog into a cave near Jericho, and found there many books, both Old Testament and other writings, and they included over two hundred psalms of David.

One also recalls an incident connected with Origen (A.D. 186–253), who was one of the great scholars of the Early Christian Church. Origen prepared the *Hexapla,* a parallel Old Testament in which on six columns to each page he placed side by side the Hebrew text, a transliteration of the Hebrew words in Greek characters, the Greek translations by Aquila and Symmachus, a new text of the Septuagint revised to harmonize with the Hebrew, and the Greek translation by Theodotion. In some books there were incorporated three other obscure Greek versions. Only the fifth column of Origen's *Hexapla* is known completely today, although in 1896 there was found at Milan a fragment of a tenth century manuscript containing the text of eleven psalms in five of the six columns, with the Hebrew column omitted but another added containing variant readings from the extra Greek versions just mentioned. A fragment containing a part of Ps. 22 in all six columns was found in the genizah (storage place where old and worn manuscripts were hidden) of the synagogue at Cairo.

But what is important for our present subject is the fact that Origen himself tells us that one of these extra Greek translations that he used was found, together with other Hebrew and Greek books, in a jar near Jericho in the reign of Antoninus, son of Severus. Eusebius (A.D. 265–340), in his *Church History,* says that Origen used in his *Hexapla,* besides the four well-known translations, three others, one of which he had indicated was found in a jar near Jericho. The cave in which the scrolls have recently been discovered is about eleven miles south of Jericho. Many caves are in this area.

Recovering the Earlier Text of the Hebrew Old Testament

Our knowledge of Hebrew manuscripts has increased greatly in recent years. The standard or received text which has largely been followed is the Masoretic Text edited by Jacob ben Chaiyim in 1524–1525. An important instrument was made available to scholars when in 1937 the third edition of R. Kittel's *Biblia Hebraica* (Hebrew Bible) was issued, using the Ben Asher edition of the Masoretic Text. It will be recalled (see p. 63) that this is the earliest known complete text of the entire Old Testament (tenth century). It is in the synagogue at Aleppo, but the manuscript there is not available. There is, however, a trustworthy copy of it in Leningrad which had been made in Cairo in A.D. 1008, and this was used in the third edition of Kittel's *Biblia Hebraica*. It was edited with care by our great contemporary Biblical scholar, Paul E. Kahle, and a period of ten years (1927–1937) was taken just for the printing of the text. This is in contrast with the sixteenth century text of Jacob ben Chaiyim, which had been produced on the basis of late and inaccurate manuscripts in a little over two years.

To help in the reconstruction of the best Hebrew text there are a number of fragments from the sixth century and later, recovered from the genizah of the old synagogue at Cairo. Besides the Hebrew texts like the Ben Asher or other texts in the Tiberian or Western tradition, there are some in the Babylonian and Yemenite tradition, with different methods of indicating the vowels. An example of the Babylonian texts is the A.D. 916 Leningrad text of the Latter Prophets (see p. 63). As a result of Kahle's researches, fragments of more than 120 different Biblical manuscripts with the Babylonian punctuation have been found, and a few with a pre-Tiberian or Palestinian punctuation system.

The general reader may find this discussion of manuscripts to be somewhat confusing, but this much must be said to give him an impression of the real progress made in the discovery and study of the manuscripts of the Old Testament. The relative scarcity of ancient Hebrew manuscripts is due largely to the synagogue custom of destroying worn copies lest they cause errors to creep in through being used in copying.

Recovering the Earlier Text of the Greek New Testament

The past half century has seen a great deal of progress in the discovery and research in early Greek manuscripts of the New Testament. The earliest Greek Bible manuscripts on skins or vellum, such as the Sinaiticus, Alexandrinus, and Vaticanus codices (see pp. 63, 64), are written in capital letters and are called uncials, and appear from the third through the tenth century. Those written in small letters in a running hand are called cursives or minuscules, and they range from the ninth to the sixteenth century.

Within the past few decades papyrus manuscripts have come to light, most of them fragmentary, providing some of our earliest examples of the Greek New Testament text. There is a small fragment of papyrus in the John Rylands Library at Manchester, England; it was acquired in 1920, but its nature was not recognized until 1934. It contains John 18:31-33, 37, 38, and belongs to the first half of the second century A.D. It is the oldest known manuscript of any part of the New Testament. Incidentally, the oldest known Biblical manuscript before the discovery of the Dead Sea Scrolls is a fragment in the John Rylands Library; it consists of parts of a roll of papyrus which came from the wrappings of a mummy. It was identified and published in 1936. On it is the Greek text of Deut. 23:24 to 24:3; 25:1-3; 26:12, 17-19; 28:31-33. There are a number of important discoveries of the Greek Old Testament, such as those in the Chester Beatty collection.

Among the extant New Testament papyri there are two leaves containing John 1:23-31, 33-41; 20:11-17, 19-25, from the third century A.D.; a part of a roll, containing Heb. 2:14 to 5:5; 10:8-22, 29 to 11:13; 11:28 to 12:17, from the late third or early fourth century; and a fragment of The Acts from the fourth century. Special attention should be called to the papyri in the Chester Beatty collection. Chester Beatty, an American resident in London, in 1931 bought from a dealer in Egypt some papyri which proved to be parts of codices of various books of the Greek Bible. They belong to the period between the second and fourth centuries. They included portions of some Old Testament manuscripts and of three New Testament manuscripts, and also of the Book of Enoch. Among the Old Testament papyri were fragments that contained portions of the books of Numbers and Deuteronomy as old as the middle of the second century; portions of two leaves of a codex of Jeremiah from near the end of the second century; and twenty-nine leaves from a codex containing Ezekiel, Daniel, and Esther, from the first half of the third century. But we are here interested in the New Testament papyri of this collection, and they belong to the third century or earlier. There are portions of thirty leaves of a codex of the Gospels and The Acts, fifty-six leaves of a codex of the Pauline Epistles (the University of Michigan has acquired thirty leaves from the same codex, and together they form nearly the complete manuscript), and ten leaves from a codex of Revelation. See also the Washington Codex of the Gospels, late third or fourth century.

The variations among the manuscripts of the New Testament may often be matters of wording. One may see illustrations of this by noting the Revised Standard Version margin, where the notation is made " Many [Some] ancient authorities read . . ." or " Many [Some] ancient authorities add. . . ." Sometimes there may be omissions of verses or longer passages in the earlier manuscripts. See the Revised Standard Version of Luke 22:43, 44, where the margin indicates that many ancient authorities omit vs. 43, 44. A well-known example is John 7:53 to 8:11, the story of the woman caught in adultery, which the Revised Standard Version puts in the margin, with a notation that most ancient authorities either omit it or insert it, with variations of the text, here, at the end of the Gospel of John, or after Luke 21:38. See also John 5:4; Mark 16:9–20; Luke 24:40.

In recent years some revision has been made in the Westcott and Hort classification of the types of New Testament texts into four families, i.e., the Syrian, the Western, the Neutral, and the Alexandrian. Some scholars speak today of Alexandrian, Western, Caesarean, Eastern, and Byzantine types of texts, representing different and somewhat localized types of text. It has been estimated that there are known today nearly 4,500 Greek manuscripts of the New

Testament, including, of course, fragments and lectionaries, ranging in date from the second to the fifteenth century.

A CRITICAL EDITION OF THE GREEK NEW TESTAMENT

There is today a great need for a critical edition of the Greek text of the New Testament incorporating the more recent discoveries and researches, and having a full and up-to-date critical apparatus. To meet this need, such a critical edition is being prepared, with the two main centers of work at Oxford and Chicago. It is called " The International New Testament Manuscripts Project." There are four permanent committees on Greek Manuscripts, Versions, Patristics, and Lectionaries, and this suggests the kinds of materials that have to be examined and compared. " Patristics " has reference to the use of the New Testament by the Early Church Fathers in quoting from the Greek or from the versions, and the lectionaries are church reading books containing portions of the Bible appointed to be read in the several days of the ecclesiastical and civil year, important for tracing the text of the New Testament during the Middle Ages.

Of particular importance for this project is a unique program of manuscript exploration carried out in 1949–1950 in the libraries of the patriarchates at Jerusalem and the library of St. Catherine's Monastery at Mt. Sinai. This involved examining the libraries and microfilming about 3,000 manuscripts in twelve languages, reproducing nearly 1,500,000 pages of text on nearly twelve miles of film. It was under the direction of Professor Kenneth Clark, Annual Professor of the American Schools of Oriental Research in Jerusalem, with the Library of Congress providing its own photographer, and about a ton of cameras, film, and other photographic equipment. The Sinai expedition was sponsored by the American Foundation for the Study of Man, and the Jerusalem work directly by the American Schools. Many types of manuscripts were microfilmed, and among them were ancient uncial copies of the Old and New Testaments, whose bearing on the textual problems will be known now for the first time. As a result of this project, through the microfilms a new vast resource will be made available to scholars, and Professor Clark comments that never before has so large and important a body of research material been presented en bloc to the world of scholarship. One may expect considerable light to be shed on the text of the New Testament when the relevant manuscripts have been examined.

The Greek of the Greek New Testament

It is now realized that the Greek of the New Testament must be compared, not with the classical or literary Greek such as that used by Plato or Aristotle, but with Koine ("common"), the contemporary Greek used by the average man all over the Greek-speaking world. This popular Greek is known principally from thousands of pieces of Greek papyri from Egypt, many of them from the first century. The recognition of the linguistic differences between Koine and literary Greek has important implications for the translation of the New Testament, and it is difficult for classically educated translators unaware of these differences to comprehend certain aspects of the meaning of the New Testament Greek. The Greek of the New Testament is not, however, uniform, some writers using a more vernacular style than others, while some may reflect a more Semitic style. Semitic influence in New Testament Greek is due largely to the fact that Aramaic was the vernacular tongue of the writers of the New Testament. A few scholars believe that the Gospels were actually originally written in Aramaic, and were later translated into Greek, but this has not received wide acceptance.

Uncertainties in the Hebrew Text

Variations in ancient authorities for the Greek text are a greater problem for the New Testament than Hebrew manuscript variations for the Old Testament. But in the Old Testament there are difficult problems of reconstruction due to corruptions in the text. Copyists' errors may make a passage so corrupt that only a conjectural reading is possible. The versions, used cautiously, may give help in recovering the original text in such cases. Likewise in the Old Testament vocabulary problems are greater than in the New Testament. Also, because the same Hebrew text may at times be susceptible to a variety of grammatical and syntactical interpretations, a number of translations of that text may be possible. How variant a translation may be made from an uncertain text may be illustrated by Prov. 26:10 as rendered by the King James Version, the American Standard Version, and the Revised Standard Version:

King James Version:
" The great *God,* that formed all *things,* both rewardeth the fool, and rewardeth transgressors."

American Standard Version:
" As an archer that woundeth all,
So is he that hireth a fool and he that hireth them that pass by."

Revised Standard Version:
" Like an archer who wounds everybody
is he who hires a passing fool or a drunkard."

The Revised Standard Version properly notes in the margin that the Hebrew text is uncertain. The progress that has been made in the understanding of Hebrew grammar is another subject that we might have discussed in this chapter, but it would perhaps be out of place in a general treatment such as this.

IMPLICATION OF TEXTUAL STUDIES

We may conclude from what we have discussed in this chapter that a fundamental problem in Bible translation is the establishment of the best possible text from which to translate. And this is by no means a simple task. We do not possess any perfect text, either of the Old Testament or the New Testament. But we certainly can reconstruct a text that is more accurate than any known in 1611, or even 1881–1885 or 1901. With the background of knowledge indicated in this chapter, we can hardly maintain that a translation is better because it is an older translation. Some may have a personal preference for an older translation because of its associations, but two questions should be asked concerning a translation: Upon what kind of text is the translation based? Given the superiority of the text upon which the translation is based, how accurate is the translation itself?

VII ✎

SOME TWENTIETH CENTURY TRANSLATIONS

THE first half of this century witnessed the appearance of a large number of new translations of the Old and New Testaments. Most of them, although not all, have been the work of individual translators. They have been made in part because the need has been felt for a translation in twentieth century English, in part because better manuscript sources have been available, and in part with the intention of producing a more accurate translation. The following discussion includes only some of the more important translations within this period. Special attention will be paid to the motives for translation, particularly as indicated in the prefaces to the translations. In general the translators used contemporary literary forms, with modern paragraphing, quotation marks, a single-column page, and with the verse numbers put in the margins; sometimes there were chapter headings and subtitles. Some translators rearranged the order of the books in accord with the date of their composition.

The Twentieth Century New Testament

It is fitting that we begin with *The Twentieth Century New Testament*. It was done by a company of about twenty scholars who represented various sections of the Christian Church but whose names were not given. A "Tentative Edition" was issued in three parts between 1898 and 1901, and a revision in 1904. It was based on the critical Greek text of Westcott and Hort (see p. 65). The preface informs us that it had its origin in the recognition of the fact that the English of the King James Version, though widely valued for its antique charm, is in many places difficult or even quite unintelligible to the modern reader. The retention of a form of English no longer in common use might suggest that the Bible had little to do with the life of today; so this new translation was an endeavor to provide the English nation with the New Testament in that form of their language which they themselves use, and to make it for the modern readers the living reality it was for its first readers. Measures of time and space, values of coins, and official titles were given in their nearest English equivalents. Passages not thought original were enclosed in square brackets. Within general subdivisions the books were arranged in what was regarded as their probable chronological order; the Gospels were thus put in the order Mark, Matthew, Luke, John. Each book was preceded with a brief, single-page introduction. Modern paragraphing, quotation marks, titles, and subtitles were used.

MOFFATT'S HISTORICAL NEW TESTAMENT

One of the most important individual translators in this period was James Moffatt, who had taught in Scotland and later came to Union Theological Seminary. Before coming to this country, he published in 1901 *The Historical New Testament*. The title page describes it as the literature of the New Testament in a new translation, arranged in the order of its literary growth and according to the dates of the documents. Besides an explanatory introduction, it contained historical tables, critical notes incorporating the results of modern research, and an appendix on problems of interpolation (secondary additions), compilation, and authorship, with introductions to the various books. Brackets indicated displaced sections or additions from a later period, and a darker type indicated passages incorporated from an earlier source. Old Testament quotations in the New Testament were put into italics. The Epistles of Paul, being the earliest books, were placed first. The translation is carefully distinguished from a revision. It is based on the critical Greek text of Nestle (1898, 1900).

WEYMOUTH'S NEW TESTAMENT

In 1903, Richard F. Weymouth, a layman and a graduate of University College, London, produced *The New Testament in Modern Speech,* edited and partly revised by E. Hampden-Cook. It is subtitled " an idiomatic translation into everyday English from the text of the Resultant Greek Testament." This "Resultant Greek Testament" was a critical Greek text based on recent editions and published by Weymouth himself. Weymouth's translation has brief introductions to the various books, modern paragraphing, quotation marks, section titles at frequent intervals, and footnotes which are largely explanations of the translation of the text. It has been a popular translation, and the first American Edition, newly revised by J. A. Robertson, was published in 1943 by The Pilgrim Press (now by Harper & Brothers).

Weymouth believed that many antiquated words and phrases were still in constant use and could appear in a modern translation. He would translate into "twentieth century English," at the same time avoiding colloquialisms to preserve the dignity of the language. His intent was not to supplant the existing versions, but to supplement them. Yet he thought that it could scarcely be doubted that someday the attempt would be renewed to produce a satisfactory English Bible which might altogether replace both the King James Version and the English Revised Version. He hoped that he might contribute some of the materials that would be "built into that far grander edifice." Weymouth, along with other twentieth century translators, was consulted by the revisers in preparing the Revised Standard Version.

FENTON'S NEW TESTAMENT

In 1895, Ferrar Fenton, a businessman, had published in London *The New Testament in Modern English,* and in 1903 he issued *The Bible in Modern English,* A. & C. Black, Ltd. It contains some strange spellings of names, and "the LORD" (or "GOD" = "Jehovah" in some translations) was rendered "Ever-living." He believed the Gospel of John to be a translation from an original Hebrew work by the apostle John, and he put this at the beginning of the New Testament. A new edition was published in 1938. It is not a particularly good translation.

MOULTON'S BIBLE

After presenting his work in a series of twenty-one publications with a single book of the Bible in each, Richard G. Moulton, Professor of Literary Theory and Interpretation at the University of Chicago, issued in 1907 the completed volume, *The Modern Reader's Bible* (The Macmillan Company), which included also the three Apocryphal books of Tobit, the Wisdom of Solomon, and Ecclesiasticus. It contained literary introductions to the books of the Bible, general notes, notes to particular books, suggestions for Bible study, and an index to the subtitled sections of the various books. Moulton attempted to illustrate by the printed form the literary form and the structure of the books of the Bible. The order of the books is rearranged to bring out " the unity of a dramatic plot." As in many of the modern translations, the poetic sections are printed as poetry, including, of course, the poetic compositions of the prophets. It is based on the English Revised Version, with the marginal readings used at discretion, and with slight changes to adapt it to modern literary structure.

THE HOLY BIBLE — AN IMPROVED EDITION

In 1913 the American Baptist Publication Society issued *The Holy Bible, Containing the Old and New Testaments, An Improved Edition*. It was based in part on the *Bible Union Version*. The American Bible Union had issued the *Bible Union New Testament* (completed in 1864) and parts of the Old Testament. Professors B. C. Taylor, W. R. Harper, J. R. Sampey, and I. M. Price worked on various portions of the Old Testament in this *Improved Edition*. J. M. P. Smith read and revised the proof of Harper's portion. Smith and Sampey were later to be among the early members of the Standard Bible Committee. The New Testament in the *Improved Edition* was the fourth edition of the *Bible Union Version* (the previous editions being those of 1864, 1865, 1891). Where the word " baptize " occurred, it was followed by the word " immerse " in parentheses. The poetic sections in the Old and New Testaments were printed as poetry, including the poetic portions of the books of the prophets. In place of the italics which the King James Version had used to indicate supplied words, brackets were used. Modern paragraphing is used, but not quotation marks. Selected footnotes provide occasional commentary.

THE RIVERSIDE NEW TESTAMENT

The Riverside New Testament (Houghton Mifflin Company, 1923) was translated by William G. Ballantine, who had taught at the Oberlin Graduate School of Theology, served as President of Oberlin College, and later became teacher at the Y.M.C.A. College in Springfield, Massachusetts. Near the beginning of the preface the translator comments that for inquirers eager to know the message of God the King James Version, " The Westminster Abbey of English Literature," is three hundred years behind the times, while the English and American revisions of it left the broad fundamental disadvantages untouched. The translation follows Nestle's Greek text. The translator acknowledges debt to Weymouth's and Moffatt's translations of the New Testament, to *The Twentieth Century New Testament,* and to the King James Version and the English and American revisions. He affirms that people have a right to have the New Testament not only in the English of the day but also in an attractive form like that of other books which they read. Verse numbers were omitted and an index at the back of the book gave the pages where persons and subjects appear. A revised edition of *The Riverside New Testament* appeared in 1934.

MOFFATT'S BIBLE

We must now return to James Moffatt. In 1913 he published in Edinburgh *The New Testament, a New Translation.* It was based on a critical Greek text edited by Hermann von Soden, of Berlin (1902–1913). In the preface Moffatt comments that he has tried to translate the New Testament exactly as one would render any piece of contemporary Greek prose. The books are arranged in the usual order, although verses or paragraphs are occasionally transposed to restore what Moffatt considers to be the original order. Thus John 3:22–30 is placed between ch. 2:12 and ch. 2:13. Footnotes call attention to such transpositions or indicate the nature of emendations or omissions in the text. This is generally recognized as an excellent translation by one of the most thorough scholars of this period.

In 1924, Moffatt issued a significant new translation of the Old Testament. He describes it as a fresh translation of the original.

Where the Hebrew text is broken or defective, or in such disrepair that plausible conjectural restoration seemed impossible, he omitted the text and inserted dots (. . .). In the poetic books a longer line of dots meant that the original text was missing or too defective to be restored. There is no indication where he has made emendations, and he thought that to try to justify the readings would have enlarged the book excessively. In rendering the divine name for which the American Standard Version had used " Jehovah," Moffatt followed the practice of the French translations and Matthew Arnold and used " the Eternal," except in the title " the LORD of hosts." Particularly in the earlier historical books, he distinguished by the use of italics and brackets one or two of the documents or sources that were used in the composition of the particular Biblical book. Double brackets denoted passages that Moffatt regarded as later additions.

Moffatt's complete Bible was issued in 1926. It has gone through many editions and is one of the most popular of the unauthorized translations. Moffatt succeeded in his intent to put his translation into effective, intelligible English, and he often caught the deeper significance of a passage where the more literal translations failed. His renderings often are more a paraphrase or free interpretation than a translation, the phraseology and sentence structure differing widely from the more traditional translations. The free renderings and the transpositions of passages and distinctions of sources make it take on the aspect of a commentary. A " Revised and Final Edition " of the Moffatt Bible was issued in 1935 (Harper & Brothers), the culmination of many printings and several revisions.

GOODSPEED'S NEW TESTAMENT

Moffatt's Bible, Goodspeed's New Testament, and a translation of the Old Testament under the editorship of J. M. P. Smith (*An American Translation*) are perhaps the best-known modern-speech translations today. In 1923, Edgar J. Goodspeed at the invitation of the University of Chicago Press issued *The New Testament, An American Translation,* based on the Westcott and Hort text. Goodspeed believed that the simple direct English of everyday expression was the appropriate medium of New Testament translation, since it was written originally, not in classical or literary Greek, but in the common language of everyday life. His translation is in the American idiom, in contrast with that of Moffatt, which has been described as modern colloquial British English. In the first edition the verse and chapter numbers were not indicated, save by a note at the bottom of the page which gave the over-all figure for the chapter and verses included on the page. Goodspeed, like Moffatt, took into consideration the results of recent studies of the text, grammar, vocabulary, and interpretation of the New Testament, including the more recent manuscript discoveries. His translation has, of course, paragraphing, quotation marks, etc. Pronouns such as " thee," " thou," " ye," etc., and such verbal forms as " makest," " hast," and " doth," are avoided, even when the Deity is addressed. Moffatt, Weymouth, and others had retained such forms in the latter instance, as the contemporary language of prayer.

The Smith-Goodspeed Bible

Goodspeed's New Testament has become a part of an understandably popular Bible published by the University of Chicago Press. *The Old Testament, An American Translation,* edited by J. M. P. Smith, was first published in 1927. Four translators were responsible for translation of different portions of it. They were T. J. Meek, of the University of Toronto; Leroy Waterman, of the University of Michigan; A. R. Gordon, of McGill University in Montreal; and J. M. P. Smith, of the University of Chicago.

The motivation of the translation is evident from the editor's preface, in which it is pointed out that the most urgent demand for a new translation comes from the field of Hebrew scholarship, due to increased knowledge in vocabulary and syntax and modern studies of textual problems. The translation aims at being easily understood wherever English is spoken, and it tries to be American " in the sense that the writings of Lincoln, Roosevelt, and Wilson are American."

Paragraphing, quotations, poetic forms, etc. are employed. Subject titles very helpful to the reader are added at proper points, and at the top of alternate pages are headings taken from the subject titles. When first published, there was an appendix of ninety-one pages listing emendations followed where the Hebrew text did not make satisfactory sense. " Thou," " thee," etc., and corresponding verbal forms were retained only in language of address to God. The reading " LORD (GOD) " of the King James Version was adopted, rather than " Jehovah." Particularly effective are the poetic sections, especially The Psalms and Job. Although by no means a literal translation, it is not paraphrastic like Moffatt's Bible. Its dependence on the traditional versions is much more evident, and much of its phraseology has a familiar ring.

Partly because various parts were translated by different persons, the first edition was not of uniform quality. Some parts were done better than others, and the literary style of the translators naturally differed. Although the preface argues that this should not be regarded as a defect, it is a feature best avoided and best remedied by having the translation the product of a committee working closely together. Subsequent editing of this translation by T. J. Meek has made more uniform the general excellence and literary style of the translation.

In 1931, Goodspeed's New Testament was published together with this Old Testament translation as *The Bible, An American Translation*. Selections from this were issued in 1933 as *The Short Bible, An American Translation,* with the various books arranged in chronological order of their composition, and with each book preceded by a brief introduction. Because of limitations of space, nine books were omitted in their entirety. Fifteen verses from the Apocryphal book of Ecclesiasticus were included. In 1939 the University of Chicago Press issued *The Complete Bible, An American Translation,* which consisted of T. J. Meek's revision of the translation of the Old Testament, Goodspeed's New Testament, and an important new translation of the Apocryphal books by Goodspeed.

THE CENTENARY NEW TESTAMENT

We have seen that in the nineteenth century a woman, Julia Smith, had made a mechanical translation of the Bible. In 1885, Mrs. Helen Spurrell, of London, had made a translation of the Old Testament, having learned Hebrew when she was more than fifty years old. She described it as a translation " from the *unpointed*

Hebrew; that being *the Original* Hebrew," and added footnotes containing variant manuscript readings, ancient versions sometimes followed, and alternate translations. More important was the appearance in 1924, in the period with which we are here concerned, of *The Centenary Translation of the New Testament*. It was published in Philadelphia, in commemoration of one hundred years of work of the American Baptist Publication Society in distributing, translating, and publishing Bibles. The translator was Mrs. Helen Barrett Montgomery, of Rochester, New York, a graduate of Wellesley and a leader in the American Baptist Church. Her aim was "a translation in the language of everyday life" which did not "depart too much from translations already familiar and beloved." It was accompanied by a brief introduction to each book, with a title given to each chapter and subtitles given to paragraphs.

THE BERKELEY VERSION

Gerrit Verkuyl, who for many years was with the Board of Christian Education of the Presbyterian Church, U.S.A., published in 1945 in Berkeley, California, the *Berkeley Version of the New Testament* (Gillick and Co.), based on Tischendorf's Greek text (see p. 65). Other Greek texts and translations in various languages were also consulted. It was motivated by a desire to use reliable Greek manuscripts and to use the language in which we live and think, rather than that of our ancestors, who expressed themselves differently. The translator later wrote that his aim was a translation less interpretive than Moffatt's, more cultured in language than Goodspeed's translation, more American than Weymouth's translation, and more free from the King James Version than is the Revised Standard Version. The translation is accompanied by a brief commentary in the footnotes. A translation of the Old Testament is in process by a group of " conservative " scholars.

THE BIBLE IN BASIC ENGLISH

An interesting recent translation is *The Basic Bible,* published in 1950, containing the Old and New Testaments in Basic English. *The New Testament in Basic English* had been issued separately in 1941. Basic English is a simplified English vocabulary in which only 850 words are used to give the sense of anything that may be said in English. For the purposes of putting the Bible into Basic English the list of words had been increased to one thousand. The translation was made by a committee under the direction of S. H. Hooke, Professor Emeritus of Old Testament in the University of London, with the final translation reviewed by a committee formed by the Syndics of the Cambridge University Press. The translation was thus something more than a " stunt."

The prefaced note acknowledges that the narrow limits of the word list of Basic English often made it hard to keep the Basic English completely parallel with the Hebrew and Greek from which the translation was made, and that from time to time some of the more delicate shades of sense have not been covered. But it asserts that the power and music of the language of the King James Version occupy so much of the reader's attention that these more delicate shades are there overlooked by the reader. The translation was not made to compete with the King James Version, but rather that its straightforwardness and simple qualities might give it an independent value. Within the language limitations imposed it is a good translation, but it must be acknowledged that a translator often wishes that the English language were more varied and versatile than it is. This artificial limitation puts a strain on both the translator and the reader. The translation makes no attempt at modern paragraphing, and there is no distinction made in the printing of prose and poetry.

JEWISH TRANSLATIONS

While the Hebrew Old Testament continues to hold the central place in the synagogue services, English-speaking Jews have recognized the need for the Bible in their vernacular. Important translations were made by Isaac Leeser (1853) in America, and by A. Benisch (1851–1856) and M. Friedlander (1884) in England. In 1917 the Jewish Publication Society issued a translation of the Old Testament in English, called *The Holy Scriptures According to the Masoretic Text, a New Translation.* The preface recalls a story told by the rabbis that Joshua had the law written upon the stones of the altar (see Josh. 8:32) in Hebrew and in seventy other languages, all the languages of mankind.

This 1917 translation was made with the aid of previous versions and constant consultation of Jewish authorities. It was the work of a board of editors, who took seven years for the task, meeting together for a total of 160 days, with decisions settled by majority vote. It was the first group translation by men representative of Jewish learning. Considerable use was made of English translations from Tyndale to the American Standard Version, and it possesses much of the rhythm and diction of the Protestant versions " in the tradition." It has been called " a Synagogal adaptation of the Anglican Old Testament." The order of the books follows that in the Hebrew Bible. Poetic form is recognized, and modern paragraphing and quotation marks are used. At numerous points the translation is an improvement over the versions consulted.

CATHOLIC TRANSLATIONS

The Roman Catholic Church has also expressed increasing interest in the reading and translation of the Scriptures. In 1898, Pope Leo XIII granted to the faithful three hundred days' indulgence (i.e., the equivalent of three hundred less days to be spent in purgatory) if they would read the Gospels for at least fifteen minutes with veneration and as spiritual reading. In 1920, Pope Benedict XV affirmed that the faithful should be urged to read daily the Gospels, The Acts, and the Epistles. There began to appear, in 1913, *The Westminster Version of the Sacred Scriptures.* The New Testament was finished in 1935 (Longmans, Green & Company, Inc.) and a small edition of the translation was issued in 1948. Only a few of the books of the Old Testament have been completed and published. The project is a translation from the original Greek and Hebrew, with introductions and explanatory notes. It is under the general editorship of Father Cuthbert Lattey.

C. J. Callan and J. A. McHugh in 1937 edited *The New Testament of Our Lord and Saviour Jesus Christ* (The Macmillan Company), translated out of the original Greek by Father F. A. Spencer, the son of an Episcopal clergyman and a convert to Catholicism. Spencer had published in 1901 a translation of the Gospels, and completed the entire New Testament just shortly before his death. The Vulgate readings when different from the Greek were given in brackets or in footnotes.

In 1941 a group of Catholic scholars under the patronage of the Episcopal Committee of the Confraternity of Christian Doctrine issued a new translation of the New Testament from the Latin Vulgate. It was a revision of the Challoner-Rheims Version (see p. 47). The stated motivation for the revision was the loss of value in the older version because of progressive changes in the English language. It was made by some twenty-seven translators, and took five years to complete. It takes into consideration the evidences for the more ancient text of the Vulgate, and the footnotes call attention to the variations in the Greek text, although the Greek is not followed in preference to the Latin. Modern paragraphing is used and poetic forms are recognized. It was done with the confidence that it would advance the reading and appreciation of the New Testament. In a letter at the beginning the president of the Pontifical Commission expresses confidence that the means of its distribution will insure easily and quickly the spread of the written Word of God in Catholic homes in America, and hopes that the translation will be welcome everywhere. The general attitude expressed in the introductory material is in sharp contrast with that in the original Rheims and Douai Version, although of course the Roman Catholic Church is accredited with sole rights as the guardian and dispenser of the Holy Scripture.

A project is under way for the translation of the Old Testament from the original Hebrew by members of the Catholic Biblical Association of America, sponsored by the Episcopal Committee of the Confraternity of Christian Doctrine. The project is in conformity with a pronouncement of Pope Pius XII in an encyclical letter in 1943. The goal of the translators in rendering the Word of God into the vernacular is rigorous fidelity to the meaning of the original, expressed in simple and intelligible language. The book of Genesis appeared in 1948 and The Psalms (with the Canticles of the Roman Breviary) in 1950. Brief introductions and critical footnotes with interpretations in conformity with Catholic doctrine are used. This promises to be an excellent and important translation.

Ronald A. Knox has made an important Catholic translation of the Bible, including the Apocrypha, from the Vulgate: *The New Testament of Our Lord and Saviour Jesus Christ* (Sheed & Ward, Ltd., 1944), and *The Old Testament* (Sheed & Ward, Ltd., 1948–1950, in two volumes). The New Testament was translated at the request of the archbishops and bishops of England and Wales, and the Old Testament at the request of the cardinal archbishop of Westminster. The translation of the Old Testament books was made with constant reference to the Hebrew text and consultation of the Septuagint. In a few cases where the Vulgate yields no tolerable sense, or has a sense inconsistent with the passage or verse as a whole, the Hebrew is followed, with a literal translation of the Vulgate in the footnotes. Modern paragraphing is used, but no recognition made of poetic forms. Archaic pronouns and verbal forms are retained.

Catholic Biblical interests are further illustrated in the preparation of a definitive and authoritative text of the Latin Vulgate. The need for this was expressed by Pope Pius X, and in 1907 the Commissio Pontificia, a group of Benedictine monks, was appointed to do the work. Nine volumes have appeared, including the books from Genesis through Ezra, and Tobias, Judith, Esther, and Job. It is a thorough work, and it is important that the best possible text of the Vulgate be determined. Compare this with the project for the critical text of the Greek New Testament noted on p. 86.

TRANSLATIONS TO COME

In 1947 a project was begun in Great Britain to make a translation of the Bible that would be an entirely new translation, not a revision of any of the existing versions, and which would have the support of all the principal non-Roman-Catholic Churches. A representative supervisory Joint Committee was set up by the main religious bodies, with the Bishop of Truro as chairman. The translation committee, whose members were not necessarily on the Joint Committee, were divided into four panels. Three of the panels are responsible for preparing the Old Testament, the New Testament, and the Apocrypha, respectively. The fourth panel consists of literary advisers whose concern is the literary excellence of the translation. It is planned to produce a translation that may receive general recognition as an authoritative second version alongside the King James Version. The general director, Professor C. H. Dodd, has said that it is hoped that this may remove in some measure a real barrier between a large proportion of his fellow countrymen and the truth of the Holy Scriptures.

Under the sponsorship of Dropsie College for Hebrew and Cognate Learning in Philadelphia, a new translation of the Apocrypha and pseudepigrapha (= other late writings, such as the Book of Enoch, the Book of Jubilees, the Testament of the Twelve Patriarchs, etc.) is being made. The work bears the title *Jewish Apocryphal Literature,* with a single book in each volume, presenting both the text and the translation. It includes also introductory material, commentary, and textual variants. It is expected to take about ten years, and the editor in chief of the series is Professor Solomon Zeitlin, of Dropsie College.

VIII ✒

MAKING THE REVISED STANDARD VERSION

A New Translation Needed

No translation of the Bible is final, even though it may be more accurately translated in more understandable language than any preceding translation. It is with this in mind that we might use as the keynote to this and the following chapter these words from the preface of the Bishops' Bible: "No offence can justly be taken for this new labour, nothing prejudicing any other man's judgment by this doing: nor yet hereby professing this to be so absolute a translation, as that hereafter might follow no other that might see that, which as yet was not understanded . . . Who can doubt but that such things as remain yet unknown in the gospel, shall be hereafter made open to the latter wits of our posterity, to their clear understanding?"

The numerous twentieth century translations described in the preceding chapter have not satisfied the need of the churches for a version that would incorporate the results of present-day knowledge of Biblical languages and manuscripts. Some of these translations have been used occasionally or often by ministers in church services. For the larger part the intention of the translators has not been to provide a version that would be a substitute for those already in use in the churches. And the translations have not been officially initiated by the Church, but rather have been the projects of individual scholars or groups of scholars who have realized the need for a more faithful and understandable representation of the Word of God. Those that are the work of a single person represent ultimately the viewpoint of a single person.

In two ways these translations have laid the groundwork for a more adequate version that does have Church sponsorship. In the first place, they have accustomed the people of our day to the idea of a new translation that avoids obscure and sometimes unintelligible English. They have dramatized how the meaning of certain Biblical passages may be made richer and clearer in a new translation. People in many churches have become used to having a new translation used in the pulpit. The people of today are much more ready to receive a new Church-sponsored translation than were the churchgoers of the days when the King James Version was issued. In the second place, these twentieth century translations all have something to contribute to a present-day translation made under the guidance and direction of the Churches by scholars representative of the Churches. A group of scholars making a new authorized translation would very naturally consult the modern translations, even though their translation procedures and purposes might be different. Actually, among the translators of the Revised Standard Version were Professors Moffatt, Goodspeed, and Waterman, who have been mentioned among the translators in the preceding chapter.

A version that is made for the Churches should be a co-operative project with many different Church bodies participating. Keeping in mind excellency of scholarship, the translators should be selected from several denominations and include some with special concerns for the use of the Bible in worship and religious education. John Eadie, in criticizing the Bishops' Bible for its want of uniformity in its various parts, comments that " it is only by earnest deliberation, the constant exchange of critical opinion, and the survey of a term or an idiom on all sides, that a good and popular version can be formed." Eadie points out that the Genevan Bible was the first to spring from " collegiate labor," i.e., co-operative labor of colleagues. A new translation suitable for use in the churches, which incorporates the values in translations that have proved themselves by use in the churches, should not be a completely fresh translation. It should be made " in the tradition." In other words, it should be a revision. While appealing to individuals for personal and home use, it should retain the dignity and grandeur, the rhythm and phrasing, that make it sound not strange in the litanies of the church service. It must be something more than a colloquial translation, and it should not seek new and striking phrases just for the sake of novelty.

The Revised Standard Version is designed to meet the requirements of such a Church-sponsored translation. It is the fifth authorized version in the history of the making of the English Bible. The other four are the Great Bible (1539), the Bishops' Bible (1568), the King James Version (1611), and the English Revised and American Standard Versions (1881–1885, 1901). The last two may be classed as one, since the American Standard Version was a variant of the English Revised Version.

THE BEGINNINGS OF THE REVISED STANDARD VERSION

It will be recalled that the American Standard Version had been copyrighted by Thomas Nelson & Sons in order to protect it from unauthorized changes. In 1928 the copyright was transferred to what was then known as the International Council of Religious Education. This was an organization in which the educational boards of forty major Protestant denominations of the United States and Canada were associated. It was a representative body of American Protestantism. The International Council of Religious Education established the American Standard Bible Committee (now known as the Standard Bible Committee) to be the custodian of the text of the American Standard Version. It was a committee of scholars, and they were authorized to undertake a revision of the translation if it were thought advisable. The Committee met for five meetings in 1930–1932, but it was not until 1937 that by vote of the International Council of Religious Education the revision was authorized and the long task begun.

The action taken by the International Council affirmed the conviction of the need for a revision " which embodies the best results of modern scholarship as to the meaning of the Scriptures, and expresses this meaning in English diction which is designed for use in public and private worship and preserves those qualities which have given to the King James Version a supreme place in English literature." It defined the translators' task as " the revision of the present American Standard Edition of the Bible in the light of the results of modern scholarship, this revision to be designed for use in public and private worship, and to be in the direction of the simple, classic English style of the King James Version." Not less than three and not more than five of the fifteen members of the Committee were to be chosen with a view to their competence in English literature and their experience in the conduct of public worship or in religious education. Not less than ten or more than twelve were to be chosen for their competence in Biblical scholarship. The purpose of the new translation is well indicated by the nature of this action by the International Council of Religious Education.

It was later found necessary to increase the size of the Committee, and some replacements have had to be made during the twenty-three years that the Committee has been in existence. At present there are twenty-two members.[1] Since its beginning the chairman of the Standard Bible Committee has been Luther A. Weigle, now dean emeritus of the Yale Divinity School, a noted scholar and churchman, past-president of the Federal Council of the Churches of Christ in America, chairman of the World's Sunday School Association, and an active participant in many other interdenominational activities. James Moffatt, of Union Theological Seminary, whom we have already met in the preceding chapter, was executive secretary of the Committee until his death in 1944. He was succeeded in this position by Fleming James, dean emeritus of the School of Theology, the University of the South, Sewanee, Tennessee.

The total number who have assisted in the translation far exceeds the number of persons on the Committee. There was an advisory board representing the denominations associated with the International Council of Religious Education. The first draft of the trans-

---

[1] The present members of the Standard Bible Committee are: Luther A. Weigle, Chairman; Fleming James, Executive Secretary of the Old Testament Section; William F. Albright, Julius A. Bewer, Walter R. Bowie, Millar Burrows, H. J. Cadbury, Clarence T. Craig, George Dahl, Edgar J. Goodspeed, Frederick C. Grant, J. Philip Hyatt, William A. Irwin, Herbert G. May, James Muilenburg, Harry M. Orlinsky, Paul C. Payne, Roy G. Ross, Willard L. Sperry, Leroy Waterman, Abdel R. Wentz, Kyle M. Yates. John C. Trever is Representative of the Standard Bible Committee on the Division of Christian Education. Drs. Payne and Ross, respectively Chairman and Executive Secretary of the Division of Christian Education, are ex officio members without assignment to Sections, charged with special responsibility for matters of general policy, finance, and public relations.

lation was made available to them, and many important suggestions were received from them. In addition there was similar co-operation on the Old Testament translation from some of the members of the committee of British scholars who are engaged in the new translation project in Great Britain. The members for the Standard Bible Committee have come from more than twenty theological seminaries and universities, and the number is of course greatly increased if we include all those assisting in the translation.

On November 29, 1950, the National Council of the Churches of Christ in the United States of America was formally constituted at Cleveland, Ohio. It was a more inclusive body than the Federal Council of the Churches of Christ had been. The International Council of Religious Education became the Division of Christian Education within the National Council. The National Council through its Division of Christian Education thus came to sponsor the new translation, and has voted its approval.

TRANSLATION PROCEDURES

The Standard Bible Committee was divided into an Old Testament Section and a New Testament Section. Although a final acceptance of the completed translation of both the Old and New Testaments by a two-thirds vote of the entire Committee was required, voting on details of the translation within the respective Old Testament and New Testament Sections was by a simple majority. In case of a tie vote, the reading of the American Standard Version was retained. After some experimentation the following procedure of translation was worked out. An individual member of a Section would be asked to prepare a preliminary translation of a book. The translator was to remember that his task was not an entirely new translation, but a revision of the American Standard Version, in which changes were to be made only when dictated by considerations of scholarship or English.

Copies of this preliminary translation were mailed to other members of the Section, who studied it carefully. Then the members of the Section met together in an official meeting around a long table, and the preliminary translation was analyzed word for word or verse for verse. Each member was free to make any suggestion for alternative readings. Thus the preliminary translation served as the working model, and the draft that resulted from the deliberations of the Section, which we may call the first draft, was truly a committee product. It was often widely variant from the preliminary translation that had been submitted.

The deliberations had many of the characteristics of a seminar, save that conclusions were always determined by vote, representing a form of democracy in translation procedures. Whereas it is true that one cannot get truth by counting noses, this procedure is justified by experience as the one that results in a uniformly better translation. All the members of the Section would probably agree that the end results were immeasurably better than the preliminary translations which they had made for the Section.

The first draft was mimeographed and subject to further study by the Section. In the New Testament Section each book was studied twice more before it was finished. The Old Testament Section had a much longer job, and this first draft was given a single but thorough revision. This revision was made on the basis of more than nine hundred pages of single-spaced typewritten suggestions made by the members of the Section and by interested members of the advisory board, some suggestions also coming from the British scholars. All major problems of these " agenda " pages were considered by the Section as a whole, with lesser problems which could be answered by the general policy of the Section left to a smaller editorial subcommittee.

The meetings took place primarily in New Haven at Yale Divinity School, in New York at Union Theological Seminary, and at Hotel Northfield in East Northfield, Massachusetts. In the " Speech Room " of the Yale Divinity School at New Haven, the original of Edwin White's picture *The Signing of the Compact on the Mayflower,* looked down from the wall upon the Old Testament Section at work. Save where full-time service was given, as in the case of the executive secretary, the members of the Committee served without payment for their services, glad to be privileged to contribute time and learning to a task as vitally important as this on behalf of the Churches. Their expenses and the other expenses in connection with the preparation of the manuscript were met by advance royalties given to the International Council of Religious Education by Thomas Nelson & Sons.

The financing of such a long and large project as this and the publishing of the translation are undertakings of no small proportions. An unsuccessful effort had been made to find someone to underwrite the expenses and a syndicate of publishers to produce the new version. When Thomas Nelson & Sons agreed to do this, they were granted exclusive right to publish the Revised Standard Version for a period of ten years, after which it was to be open to other publishers. In no sense can a charge of commercialism legitimately be made in connection with the motivation of this translation. The co-operation of Thomas Nelson & Sons, first under its president, George K. Hyslop, and then under his successor, William R. McCulley, with the International Council of Religious Education has been wholehearted and generous. A testimony of appreciation is due at this point.

The sessions of the Sections at work on the translation began normally at nine A.M. and lasted until nine thirty P.M. To hasten the completion of their work near the end of their task, both the Old Testament Section and the New Testament Section met more frequently. The Old Testament Section, for instance, met for two two-weeks sessions in the summer, a seven- to ten-days session at the Christmas holidays, and an occasional week-end session. Altogether the New Testament Section met for a total of 145 days. The Old Testament required a longer time, and it met for a total of 148 days in the period from February, 1948, to June, 1951, alone, while it was working more intensively to get the work finished.

An individual translation could have been made much more quickly; opportunity had to be given for discussion of all points brought up by the members. Sometimes several hours might be spent on a single verse. Time often had to be taken for consultation of the ancient and modern versions and the commentaries. Even when the meaning of a passage had been decided upon, there might be lengthy discussion of the best possible English phrasing to represent that meaning. Often it was a choice, not between just two possible translations of a word or sentence, but among several alternatives, each of which might be warmly supported by various members of the Section. Serious consideration had to be given to the written suggestions of corresponding members who were not present to defend their views. Parallel passages in other parts of the Bible had to be looked up to see how a word under discussion had been translated at earlier meetings in similar contexts. Numerous word studies were made by Professor James between meetings to see how the same words in similar contexts had been translated. Of course the time spent in the meetings was only a small proportion of the time the members spent in the work, for it took many hours of private study between meetings.

The Revised Standard Version of the New Testament

The last meeting of the New Testament Section was at Northfield, Massachusetts, on August 15–29, 1943, when the manuscript was entrusted to a smaller editorial committee to prepare it for the press. Mimeographed copies had been sent to the members of the Old Testament Section, to secure their approval, as later similar copies of the Old Testament translation were to be sent to the New Testament Section, for the completed translation had to have the approval of the entire Committee by a two-thirds majority.

On February 11, 1946, eight years after the revision had begun, the Revised Standard Version of the New Testament was officially issued at an impressive ceremony of unusual historic significance at Columbus, Ohio. At that time Dean Luther A. Weigle presented the first copy of the Revised Standard Version to the International Council of Religious Education, and to Harold E. Stassen, president of the International Council of Religious Education, he presented the second copy of the new translation. In his address at the time Dean Weigle said: " We do not imagine that the King James Version will cease to be used because this revision has been made. We have not thought, moreover, of discontinuing the publication of the American Standard Version. Each has its use, the first as a great literary and religious classic and the second as a meticulously literal word-for-word translation. It is our hope, however, that the Revised Standard Version may quickly come to be used by ministers and by people generally, for reading and meditation, for teaching, preaching, and Christian religious education, and in public and private worship. . . . We sorely need this direct, vital phrasing of the Word of God in language that can readily be understood by the people of our time." One of the translators, Professor Clarence T. Craig, of Oberlin Graduate School of Theology, now dean of Drew Theological Seminary, was granted leave of absence from teaching to interpret the translators' work to the churches.

The New Testament was published with punctuation, quotation marks, and paragraphing in accordance with modern usage, and with a single-column page. Verse numbers were made less conspicuous and put in smaller type raised above the line. The book was bound in a blue cover, and the general form and clear type has proved very popular. Since its first printings it has appeared in various sizes and colors, some in the more traditional black binding. A brief preface of four pages explained the origin of the translation and reasons for it. It is affirmed that men need the Word of God in our time as never before, and that that Word must not be disguised in phrases that are no longer clear or are hidden under words that have lost their meaning. Along with the translation, taking the place of a more extended preface such as that in the King James Version, there was issued a small book of seventy-two pages entitled "An Introduction to the Revised Standard Version of the New Testament," written by members of the New Testament Section to make clear to the readers the principles that guided this revision.

The reception of the new translation exceeded the expectation of the publishers. The first printing was quickly sold out. Around two million copies have now been sold. An important publication project in connection with the Revised Standard Version was the issuance of *Gospel Parallels, A Synopsis of the First Three Gospels,* under the supervision of Professors H. J. Cadbury, F. C. Grant, and C. T. Craig (Thomas Nelson & Sons, 1949), which used the text of the new translation. The Synoptic Gospels (i.e., Matthew, Mark, and Luke) were printed in parallel columns for comparison, with the parallels in the Gospel of John also noted, and also alternative readings from the manuscripts and from noncanonical parallels such as the Apocryphal Gospel of Peter and the Gospel According to the Hebrews.

THE REVISED STANDARD VERSION COMPLETED

In the meantime the work on the Old Testament continued. The last meeting of the Old Testament Section was on June 12–26, 1951. The session on June 26 marked the completion of fourteen years of work by the Old Testament Section. James Moffatt had died just seven years less one day before, and William R. Taylor, of Toronto, who had been with the Committee since 1931, had died on February 24, 1951. Four of the members of the Section, Weigle, Burrows, James, and May, continued to work at New Haven throughout July and August to deal with translation details committed to them by the Section and to prepare the remaining manuscript for the printers. Part of the manuscript had been in the hands of the printers as early as the preceding April, and the printer's proof of some of it had already been received. On August 31, which marked the last gathering of this editorial subcommittee and the last group meeting of any part of the Section, Professor James conducted a simple service of thanksgiving, offering a prayer of gratitude and reading the Twenty-third Psalm and the fifty-fifth chapter of Isaiah in the newly completed version.

The Standard Bible Committee does not cease to exist with the completion of this task, for it continues as the representative of the National Council of Churches of Christ to have the oversight of the text of the Revised Standard Version.

The date for the publication of the completed Bible is September 30, 1952. The first printing consists of almost 1,000,000 volumes; 825,000 of these are volumes of the complete Bible with a two-column page, and there will also be 50,000 two-volume sets of the Old Testament in single-column page to be companion volumes of the Revised Standard New Testament in similar popular form. The publication is said to be the greatest order ever placed for a full-sized book by a commercial publishing house. It has been estimated that the first run requires more than 1,000 tons of paper, 2,000 gallons of ink, 140 tons of binder's board, 10 tons of type metal, 71 ½ miles of forty-inch cloth, 18,750,000 yards of thread, and 20,000,000 square inches of 23-karat gold leaf which would pave a street 24 feet wide and nearly a mile long. The volumes stacked in a pile would reach

24 miles into the heavens. This is not to be taken as an illustration of American love for bigness, but rather is some indication of the confident expectation of welcome reception of the new translation. On September 30 specially bound copies will be presented to selected religious leaders at 3,000 simultaneous interdenominational gatherings across the continent.

But the project is important, not because of its size, but rather because it is the expression of the need of the churches for the Word of God in as accurate a translation and as understandable a form as is possible. The observances on September 30 and throughout Religious Education Week (September 28 to October 5) are for the purpose of dedicating Protestant Christians to a renewed interest in the Bible and its message. The theme of the observance is " The Word of Life in Living Language." It is a Church-wide project. It is expected that increasingly the Revised Standard Version will be used both in the homes and in various aspects of church life.

One of the first great religious publication ventures to make use of the Revised Standard Version is a twelve-volume commentary series called *The Interpreter's Bible,* being published by the Abingdon-Cokesbury Press, involving 146 writers and editors and representing a million dollar investment by the publishers. In it the King James Version and the Revised Standard Version are printed in parallel columns. We may expect to find the Revised Standard Version coming into common use in classrooms, Sunday school lesson materials, hymnals, pulpit Bibles, devotional literature, religious journals, and many other places.

IX

THE WORD OF LIFE IN LIVING LANGUAGE

Differences Between Seventeenth Century and Twentieth Century English

THE special values of the Revised Standard Version may in part be appreciated through comparison with the King James Version. Such comparisons as we shall make here are not to be taken as criticisms detracting from the virtues of the King James Version. These virtues have been tested through the centuries. Nor can the translators of a version made in 1611 be blamed for the fact that changes in the English language have made their translation occasionally obscure and subject to misunderstanding by a twentieth century reader. Someday twentieth century English will be considered archaic to the same extent. And we cannot condemn the translators of the King James Version for not using the better manuscript sources that are now known. Someday there will doubtless be available better manuscripts than those upon which the Revised Standard Version is based.

But the Revised Standard Version, by virtue of the fact that it represents the scholarship of the twentieth century and avoids the obscurities now inevitable in English of the seventeenth century and earlier, does have great advantages over the earlier authorized versions. Weigle (*The English New Testament from Tyndale to the Revised Standard Version,* pp. 149–152) has listed 184 words in the King James Version of the New Testament that are likely to mislead a reader because they have changed their meaning, and he does not include words and expressions which, while they are archaic or obsolete, may still be understood. T. L. O. Davies (*Bible English,* London, 1875) has collected together hundreds of words in the King James Version that have an out-of-date form, that have lost some of their original meaning, that have changed their meaning although still in use, that have contracted or enlarged their meaning, that have degenerated or improved their meaning, or that have altogether passed out of use. It is hardly practical for a modern reader to keep beside him a dictionary of such words as he reads the Bible. And yet that is what a reader would have to do if he would know just what the translators of the 1611 version intended to say. The general reader is usually not aware of the extent to which misunderstanding is possible until he has noted a few examples such as the following.

Using the Vocabulary of Today

"Conversation" used to carry the meaning of "conduct." Where K.J.V. reads, "To slay such as be of upright conversation," in Ps. 37:14, the reference is not to proper speech; R.S.V. reads, "To slay those who walk uprightly" (compare also A.S.V.). Instead of the familiar K.J.V. words, "Let your conversation be without covetousness," in Heb. 13:5, R.S.V. gives in contemporary English, "Keep your life free from love of money" (compare A.S.V.).

"Purchased" is found in K.J.V. in the general sense of "acquire," as in Ps. 78:54, "This mountain which his right hand had purchased." The R.S.V. renders, "The mountain which his right hand had won" (cf. A.S.V. "gotten"). The more familiar K.J.V. phrase in I Tim. 3:13, "Purchase to themselves a good degree," has nothing to do with academic diplomas, but rather it means, "Gain a good standing for themselves," as in R.S.V. (see also A.S.V.). The word "degree" is also obscure, being used in the sense of "position" or "standing."

"Quicken," meaning "to give life," and "the quick," meaning "the living," and "quick," meaning "alive," are archaisms. It would be easy to misunderstand Ps. 119:25 in K.J.V., "Quicken thou me according to thy word," but R.S.V. makes it clear with, "Revive me according to thy word." Likewise the meaning of K.J.V., "And you hath he quickened," in Eph. 2:1, is clarified by R.S.V., "And you he made alive." Psalm 55:15 is not only apt to be misunderstood in K.J.V., but to be thought poor grammar when it is rendered, "Let them go down quick into hell," but it means, "Let them go down to Sheol alive," as in R.S.V. See also Acts 10:42, where we find in the K.J.V. the familiar, "Judge of quick and dead," but R.S.V. renders it, "Judge of the living and the dead."

A little-used meaning of "curious" is "wrought with care." Compare the latin *curiosus,* "careful." This meaning is intended in Ps. 139:15, where K.J.V. translated, "Curiously wrought in the lowest parts of the earth." The R.S.V. puts it in more common contemporary English, "Intricately wrought in the depths of the earth." In K.J.V. the phrase, "To devise curious works," in Ex. 35:32, might be taken in an unintended sense, and R.S.V. brings out the meaning with "To devise artistic designs." Compare how "careless" is used to mean "free from care" in Judg. 18:7 in K.J.V., or how "presently" is used in I Sam. 2:16 to mean "immediately," or how "unspeakable" appears in II Cor. 9:15 as "inexpressible" in R.S.V., i.e., "Thanks be to God for his inexpressible gift!" A.S.V. kept "unspeakable."

One does not hear the word "privily" used today, and "Whoso privily slandereth his neighbour" in Ps. 101:5 in K.J.V. requires several changes to make it accord with current speech. Thus R.S.V. renders it, "Him who slanders his neighbor secretly." We would probably not misunderstand, "Then Herod, when he had privily called the wise men," in Matt. 2:7 in K.J.V., but the present-day reader would find more pleasing the phrasing of R.S.V., "Then Herod summoned the wise men secretly."

Two words that bear a meaning so strange to modern ears that the reader of K.J.V. is conscious of something wrong, even though he may not know what it is, are "let" and "prevent." "Let" is sometimes used in the sense of "prevent," and "prevent" may be used to mean "come before," or "precede." We might completely misunderstand, "I will work and who shall let it?" in Isa. 43:13. It means, as in R.S.V. (see also A.S.V.), "I work, and who can hinder it?" So also, "I purposed to come unto you, (but was let hitherto,)" in Rom. 1:13, K.J.V., is to be interpreted as, "I have often intended to come to you (but thus far have been prevented)" in R.S.V. (compare A.S.V.). Compare also, "Shall not prevent them which are asleep" in K.J.V. in I Thess. 4:15 with R.S.V., "Shall not precede those who have fallen asleep" (compare A.S.V.).

When we read in Isa. 10:28, " He hath laid up his carriages," those of us who remember horse-and-buggy days are apt to visualize wagons being put into a barn. But the word " carriages " used to be employed to indicate that which one carried, and so R.S.V. (see also A.S.V.) reads, " He stores his baggage." There is no strong-man action implied in Acts 21:15 as K.J.V. had it, " We took up our carriages." It means only, " We made ready," as in R.S.V., or, " We took up our baggage," as in A.S.V.

Many other examples of this kind of thing could be given. The reader himself can look up the following passages: Gen. 30:37 (K.J.V. " pilled " = R.S.V. and A.S.V. " peeled "); Ex. 26:6 (K.J.V. " taches " = R.S.V. and A.S.V. " clasps "); Ex. 28:11 (K.J.V. " ouches " = R.S.V. and A.S.V. " settings "); Josh. 9:5 (K.J.V. " clouted " = R.S.V. and A.S.V. " patched "); I Sam. 21:13 (K.J.V. " scrabbled " = R.S.V. " make marks "); II Kings 22:4 (K.J.V. " sum the silver " = R.S.V. " reckon the amount of the money "); Job 41:18 (K.J.V. " neesings " = R.S.V. and A.S.V. " sneezings "); Isa. 14:23 (K.J.V. " besom of destruction " = R.S.V. " broom of destruction "); Isa. 43:17 (K.J.V. " extinct " = R.S.V. " extinguished "); Jer. 51:23 (K.J.V. " husbandman " = R.S.V. " farmer "). One will also find in the King James Version such words as " bolled," " knops," " hoised," " marishes," " divers," " bewray," " ambassage," etc. The American Standard Version corrected some of these archaisms, but it left others of them untouched.

" BIBLE ENGLISH "

As a result of phrasing and forms of words that are not in common use today, we tend to think of a special Bible English. When we put on church plays, we have the actors speak this special English as though this is the way people used to speak in Biblical days. We do not stop to think that this Bible English is to a large extent just the way in which people spoke when the King James translation was made. This Bible English, which may also in part be due to a literal translation of Hebrew idiomatic expressions, tends to give an atmosphere of unreality, as though the people of Biblical days lived in a world different from that in which we live. Now it is true that the culture of Old and New Testament times differed at many points from American or English culture of today. But that difference is not the difference between Elizabethan and modern English. And the world in which the Hebrew prophets and Jesus lived was not unreal. The Hebrew law, the oracles of the prophets, the teachings of Jesus, and the letters of Paul were for people facing problems in tangible and concrete life situations. We may take the Word of God in the Bible more seriously if we appreciate this.

Part of " Bible English " is the regular use of the pronouns " thee," " thou," " thy," " thine," and " ye," and verbal forms which have such endings as " -est " or " -edst." There is one place where such pronouns and verbal forms are at home today, and that is in the language of prayer. For this reason many modern versions, including the Revised Standard Version, retain them in cases of address to God. Since the psalms are largely prayers or praises to God, such forms will be found there frequently. The psalms in the new translation used as responsive readings will fit naturally into the liturgy of the church service, retaining the language of prayer.

There are certain verbal forms that are not used today, such as " sware," " gat," " drave," and " tare." We also do not use " is " or " are " as auxiliaries for the perfect tense, as in " is come " or " are come " instead of " has come " or " have come." Likewise we would avoid such expressions as " wherein," " therein," " thereof," etc. The King James Version often uses " that " where we would prefer " who," and " his " where we would use " its." The English of 1611 used certain prepositions in a way not usual today. So " of " might be employed to mean " by " or " for " or " from." " Bidden of any man " in Luke 14:8 becomes in the Revised Standard Version " Invited by any one "; " Of a child " in Mark 9:21 becomes " From childhood "; " Of a long season " in Luke 23:8 becomes " long," i.e., " For a long time." " Touching " was often used to mean " concerning," and today might be taken for a verb. Thus, " For thus saith the Lord touching Shallum," in Jer. 22:11, becomes " For thus says the Lord concerning Shallum." " Touching the Almighty, we cannot find him out," in Job 37:23, might be completely misunderstood, but it means simply " The Almighty — we cannot find him," as in the Revised Standard Version. Today we also tend to use the simple " to " instead of " unto," and " on " rather than " upon."

USING NATURAL ENGLISH EXPRESSIONS

In providing a literary form more suited to the general reader the Revised Standard Version translators have tried to avoid the literal translation of Hebrew and Greek idioms which, while natural in the original languages, make an awkward English literary style. Especially noticeable in the Old Testament, but appearing also in the New Testament as a result of Semitic influence, is the almost constant use of " and " to bind sentences together. " And " may frequently best be omitted, or replaced by such words as " now," " then," " so," " but," " when," " while," " although," " that," " in order that "; or one may otherwise indicate the relationship of the sentences, sometimes subordinating one to another. " And Serug lived thirty years, and begat Nahor," in Gen. 11:22, K.J.V., may be read with the Revised Standard Version, " When Serug had lived thirty years, he became the father of Nahor." The present knowledge of Hebrew grammar makes it possible to recognize more syntactical relationships than did the translators of the King James Version.

Hebrew may also use " and " to indicate, not a different, but an identical or synonymous thought. This is dramatically illustrated in Zech. 9:9, where in the words of the King James Version the messianic King comes " lowly, and riding upon an ass, and upon a colt the foal of an ass." In the story of the Palm Sunday parade in Matt., ch. 21, this is obviously misunderstood to mean two different animals (contrast Mark, ch. 11). The meaning is as in the Revised Standard Version:

> " Humble and riding on an ass,
> on a colt, the foal of an ass."

The frequent " And it came to pass " in both the Old and the New Testament is the representation of a Semitic idiom. All that is meant by " And it came to pass, that when Isaac was old " in Gen. 27:1 is more naturally and simply expressed in English idiom in the

Revised Standard Version's "When Isaac was old." So also "in the day that" may mean only "when," as in Isa. 11:16, Jer. 11:4, etc. The constant use of "saying" before a quotation is a Hebrew idiom and generally to be avoided, and the use of quotation marks makes it doubly superfluous. "He answered and said," "He spake, and said," or, "He spake, saying," may be rendered merely, "He answered," or, "He spoke," with the quotation enclosed in quotation marks.

English usage and clarity often demand something more than a literal translation, for the symbolic usage of one language may not be that of another. Instead of "seed" we should often translate "offspring," "children," "posterity," or "descendants," as the context might suggest. "Wild beasts" may be preferable to the literal "beasts of the field." "Sons" should sometimes be rendered "children," and for such an expression as "sons of Israel" we may often best use "men of Israel," "people of Israel," or even "Israelites." The word "face" may at times better be replaced by "surface," as in "the surface of the ground," Jer. 8:2, or by "front," as in "the front of the temple" in Ezek. 41:14. Instead of "soul" the best English meaning of the Hebrew word in certain passages or contexts may be "life," "person," "spirit," "desire," "appetite," or "he," "himself," etc. For the more literal "heart" we should sometimes read "mind," or even "will," to indicate more accurately in English what the text meant to the Hebrew reader. There may also be a too literal following of the order of words; "And they will deceive every one his neighbour" in Jer. 9:5 in the King James Version is more simply expressed in the Revised Standard Version, "Every one deceives his neighbor."

CONSISTENCY AND VARIETY

Greater accuracy in translation in the Revised Standard Version has, paradoxically enough, resulted in greater consistency and greater diversity. The translators have tried to be consistent in translating the same word in similar contexts in the same way, but have not hesitated to translate the same word in different ways when the context required it. We may illustrate this with the translation of the Hebrew word *hesed* in the Old Testament.

In the King James Version this word is most often translated "mercy," but frequently also "kindness" and "loving kindness," and a few times "goodness" and "favour," with sometimes no apparent reason for the variation. The identical Hebrew words are translated "longsuffering, and of great mercy" in Num. 14:18; "longsuffering and abundant in goodness" in Ex. 34:6; "slow to anger, and of great kindness" in Neh. 9:17; Joel 2:13; Jonah 4:2; "longsuffering, and plenteous in mercy" in Ps. 86:15; "slow to anger, and plenteous in mercy" in Ps. 103:8. It is "shewest loving kindness to thousands" in Jer. 32:18, but "shewing mercy unto thousands" in Ex. 20:6. In all these instances, and whenever *hesed* is used of God, the American Standard Version has "lovingkindness." *Hesed* is a word of great theological import, and much light has been thrown on it by recent studies. For the Revised Standard Version the Old Testament Section voted to read "[show] kindness" when the reference was to a particular act of one person, "[deal] loyally" when it was a reference to a continuous kind of behavior of one person toward another, "[show] steadfast love" when referring to God's consistent behavior toward Israel, and "[show] steadfast love" (or "devotion," "fidelity," etc.) when it referred to Israel's relation to and behavior toward God. A greater number of words are used to translate *hesed* in the Revised Standard Version than in the earlier versions, but there is at the same time more consistency in similar contexts.

The American Standard Version had brought much greater consistency into the translation, but did not appreciate fully the variant meanings of some Hebrew words. This is particularly true of a word like *çedeq,* usually translated in the King James and American Standard Versions "righteousness." But in its occurrence in Job, for instance, the Revised Standard Version translates twice by "righteousness" (chs. 29:14; 36:3), but also uses "vindication" (ch. 6:29), "rightful" (ch. 8:6), and "right" (ch. 35:2). In Isa. 41:10 it is rendered "victorious," in ch. 45:19 "the truth," and in ch. 51:1, 5, 8, "deliverance."

The Hebrew word *'ebed* often means "servant," but it also often means "slave." The King James Version has the word "slave" but once in the Old Testament, i.e., Jer. 2:14, where it is in italics to show that the word is interpretative and not in the Hebrew text. But Ex. 21:1–11 or Jer. 34:8–22 and numerous other passages cannot properly be understood apart from the institution of slavery. Similarly, in contrast with the King James Version, the new translation of the New Testament gives proper recognition to the Greek word *doulos* in its meaning " slave," sometimes with a footnote, " Or, *slave,*" sometimes with the word " slave " in the text. In such passages as Eph. 6:5–9; I Tim. 6:1, 2; Col. 3:22, Paul is concerned with slave and master relationships. See also Rom. 6:16–23. The Early Christian Church was concerned about slavery, and the translation should not soften it down by translating the word as " servant " in such contexts.

LITERARY FORMS

At two points the general literary form of the Revised Standard Version is an improvement, providing a more readable text and giving aid to understanding what is written. First, in common with most other modern translations it makes use of the punctuation, paragraphing, and quotation marks that accord with present-day practice. The King James Version was overly punctuated, and a modern book would at points use a different punctuation. This is especially true of its excessive use of the comma and its use of the colon.

The quotation marks in the Revised Standard Version help the reader, especially in certain instances where it may not otherwise be clear where the quotation ends. It must be acknowledged that the Hebrew custom of shifting back and forth from direct to indirect address, especially in poetry, often makes the use of quotation marks a problem, but this should not hinder their use.

Paragraphing permits the reader more easily to see the larger sense units and follow the theme of the passage. The Bible was not written merely to provide memory verses for Sunday school lessons or texts for ministers in the pulpit. Paragraphing should help the reader to see the Bible as something more than a succession of unrelated verses, and may help the minister to see his text in its context, and so minimize the danger of misinterpretation.

THE POETRY OF THE BIBLE

A second important aspect of the general literary form of the Revised Standard Version is its representation of the poetry of the Bible. For the poetry in the New Testament, see the Magnificat of Mary in Luke 1:46–55, the prophecy of Zechariah in Luke 1:68–79, or the many quotations from the prophets as in Matt. 1:23; 2:6; 12:18–21; 13:14, 15. A rough estimate suggests that more than a third of the Old Testament is poetry. We must include not only the so-called "Poetical Books," Job, The Psalms, Ecclesiastes, Proverbs, and The Song of Solomon, but also Lamentations and the larger share of the Prophetic writings. Besides, there are numerous poems imbedded in the historical books, like the blessing of Jacob in Gen., ch. 49, the song of Moses and the Israelites in Ex., ch. 15, the oracles of Balaam in Num., chs. 23; 24, the song and blessing of Moses in Deut., chs. 32; 33, or the song of Deborah in Judg., ch. 5.

The American Standard Version had improved on the King James Version, which had no representation of the poetry, but the American Standard Version had ignored the poetry in the Prophets. The Revised Standard Version not only prints the lines of poetry as separate lines, but indents the second line of couplets and the second and third lines of tristichs (i.e., three-line units). When the members of the Old Testament Section were translating poetry, they were conscious of that fact, and concerned with transferring the poetic qualities of the original into English. Only by such a concern on the part of the translators can a really adequate translation be prepared.

Two short passages (Amos 5:23, 24; Isa. 44:23) will illustrate the clarity, force, and vividness of the prophetic oracles when the translation gives not merely the meaning of the Hebrew words but also represents something of the literary form:

> "Take away from me the noise of your songs;
>   to the melody of your harps I will not listen.
> But let justice roll down like waters,
>   and righteousness like an ever-flowing stream."

"Sing, O heavens, for the LORD has done it;
shout, O depths of the earth;
break forth into singing, O mountains,
O forest, and every tree in it!
For the LORD has redeemed Jacob,
and will be glorified in Israel."

Although scholars disagree about the nature of Hebrew meter, it is nevertheless possible to carry over into an English translation something of the rhythm of the Hebrew poetry. The fact that Hebrew poetry has no rhyme to be reproduced is a blessing to the translator. Of special significance is the care that has been taken in the Revised Standard Version in the representation of strophic or stanza division within the poems. These are not necessarily divisions of regular length, but are poetic paragraphs, and they help the reader to appreciate the thought units within the poetry.

With the more elevated poetic passages and certain narrative portions in the Old Testament that represent masterpieces of Hebrew literature we may contrast the simple and informal style of the Greek in which the New Testament is written. The Revised Standard Version reproduces both styles as adequately as it can, for the New Testament translators recognized that in general the New Testament differs from the Old Testament in literary quality.

MARGINAL NOTES

The footnotes in the Revised Standard Version are very helpful to the Biblical student, whether that student is a member of a church school class, a college, or a theological school. A variety of textual matters are to be found in these footnotes. They include such things as the meaning of personal names when it is necessary to know the meaning in order to understand the text (see Gen., ch. 30, for several of these), the transliteration of a Hebrew word when it is used in a wordplay (see Amos 8:1, 2), possible alternative translations of a word or phrase, indications of the uncertainty or obscurity of the Hebrew text, and occasionally the literal translation of the original when a very free rendering may have been necessary.

An important type of footnote is also that which indicates the support given by one or more of the ancient versions for a conjectural reading in the text, or which indicates a conjectural reading when the text is corrupt and there may be no support from the ancient versions. In such instances, where possible, the literal meaning of the Hebrew is also given in the footnotes. The indication of conjectural reconstructions of the text wherever such changes have been made is in contrast with some modern translations which leave the reader in the dark, without indicating how the text has been treated.

PROPER NAMES

The capitalization agrees with modern usage. Thus we have "Mount Zion," "Mount Carmel," "the Valley of Siddim," "the Horse Gate," etc. Such geographical names as "the Negeb" or "the Shephelah" are written as proper names, rather than translated as "the south" or "the lowland." "Pit," when a reference to Sheol or the land of the dead, is also capitalized. Perhaps to a large extent reflecting the preferences of different translators, the King James Version uses "pit" three times, "grave" thirty-one times, and "hell" thirty-one times to translate the Hebrew "Sheol," which is really a proper name and refers to the abode of the dead in the lower world. In any case "hell" gives the reader a wrong impression, for it was not thought of as a place of punishment but as the abode of all the dead. Both American Standard and Revised Standard Versions use "Sheol."

The Revised Standard Version follows the King James Version rather than the American Standard Version in the rendering of the name of the God of the Hebrews. It was probably actually pronounced "Yahweh," and the form "Jehovah," used in the American Standard Version, is the result of a misunderstanding of the Hebrew text. The vowels "e" and "o" and "a" in the Hebrew text were inserted to indicate to the reader that he should not pronounce the sacred name of God, but that he should say instead the Hebrew word for "the LORD," which contains these vowels. The tradition of rendering the name of God as "the LORD" (or GOD) goes back to before New Testament times, and would have been followed by Jesus himself. It is best to keep this tradition.

CORRELATION OF THE TWO TESTAMENTS

Despite differences in literary style and in the languages in which they were written, there should be some correlation between the translation of the Old Testament and the New Testament. Their translation is not two completely separate projects. Both Old and New Testament had to have acceptance by a two-thirds vote of the entire Standard Bible Committee. As we have seen, the Old Testament prophecies quoted in the New Testament are put in proper poetic form, comparable to that used in the Old Testament. Proper names of Old Testament characters are rendered the same in the Old and New Testaments, in contrast with the older translations. So we find in Matt., ch. 1, " Judah " instead of " Judas," " Peres " instead of " Phares," " Tamar " instead of " Thamar," " Hezron " instead of " Ezrom," etc. This is important, for many would not recognize " Ozias " as " Uzziah," or " Achaz " as " Ahaz," or " Ezekias " as " Hezekiah." So also in Matt., chs. 3; 4; 8; 12; 13; and 15, it should be made clear that the prophet quoted is Isaiah (= " Esias "), that in Acts 7:45 Stephen refers to Joshua (= " Jesus "), or in Matt. 16:14, etc., that some thought that Jesus was Elijah (= " Elias ").

Place names in the Old Testament mentioned in the New Testament, especially in quotations, should be rendered the same, and so the Revised Standard Version has " Zebulun " and "Naphthali " in Matt. 4:15, rather than the traditional " Zabulon " and " Nephthalim." In using " Holy Spirit " (with the American Standard Version) instead of " Holy Ghost," the translation is not only more in accord with modern usage, but it helps to form a link with the Old Testament, where " Spirit " rather than " Ghost " is employed; see especially Acts 1:16, where the reference is to David's time.

LITERARY STYLE

In general the Revised Standard Version steers away from Latinized words, preferring words with an Anglo-Saxon origin. The language of the new translation is not merely the language of today, for a translation to be used in both home and church must be something more than colloquial or a passing fancy. In so far as possible it uses words that are lasting and generally respected. Only thus could it accord with the instructions to move in the direction of "the simple, classic English style of the King James Version." While its literary style is not *identical* with that of the King James Version of the seventeenth century, it is hoped that it has a *comparable* twentieth century literary style. It does avoid the unfortunate stilted literary style resulting from the mechanical literalism of the English and American revisions. It also avoids their often awkward sentence structure, which was the result of following too closely the Greek or Hebrew order of words and phrases.

MEANINGFUL AND ACCURATE TRANSLATION

Many passages could be quoted where the Revised Standard Version provides both a richer and more adequate translation, as well as one less apt to be misunderstood. Many people have wondered at the statement in Rom. 8:28: "And we know that all things work together for good to them that love God." The Revised Standard Version, on the basis of a critical study of ancient Greek manuscripts, renders more probably what Paul wrote: "We know that in everything God works for good with those who love him." "Circumcision is nothing, and uncircumcision is nothing, but the keeping of the commandments of God" in I Cor. 7:19 is easily misunderstood; the Revised Standard Version reads, "For neither circumcision counts for anything nor uncircumcision, but keeping the commandments of God."

It seems strange to say, "But God be thanked, that ye were the servants of sin," etc. (Rom. 6:17), but the meaning is clarified by the rendering, "But thanks be to God, that you who were once slaves of sin," etc. Especially when read aloud we might not get the meaning of "For he hath made him to be sin for us, who knew no sin," in II Cor. 5:21, but that it is not a reference to our sinlessness is evident from the Revised Standard Version's "For our sake he made him to be sin who knew no sin." The "all" in Matt. 26:27, "Drink ye all of it," has often been misunderstood, although one used to the expression "you all" might get the meaning; it is properly rendered, "Drink of it, all of you." "Just" does not mean "mere" in Luke 20:20, where the spies "feign themselves just men "; the American Standard Version has "righteous" and the Revised Standard Version "who pretended to be sincere."

We may conclude by comparing two brief passages from the Revised Standard Version with the rendering in the King James Version, that the reader may see for himself how fresh meanings and new values may be found in the new translation.

Ps. 119:147, 148, K.J.V.:

"I prevented the dawning of the morning, and cried: I hoped in thy word. Mine eyes prevent the night watches, that I might meditate in thy word."

R.S.V.:

> "I rise before the dawn and cry for help;
>   I hope in thy words.
> My eyes are awake before the watches of the night
>   that I may meditate upon thy promise."

Nahum 3:2-4, K.J.V.:

"The noise of a whip, and the noise of the rattling of the wheels, and of the prancing horses, and of the jumping chariots.

The horseman lifteth up both the bright sword and the glittering spear: and there is a multitude of slain, and a great number of carcases; and there is none end of their corpses; they stumble upon their corpses.

Because of the multitude of the whoredoms of the wellfavoured harlot, the mistress of witchcrafts, that selleth nations through her whoredoms, and families through her witchcrafts."

R.S.V.:

> "The crack of whip, and rumble of wheel,
>   galloping horse and bounding chariot!
> Horsemen charging,
>   flashing sword and glittering spear,
> hosts of slain,
>   heaps of corpses,
> dead bodies without end —

they stumble over the bodies!
And all for the countless harlotries of the harlot,
    graceful and of deadly charms,
who betrays nations with her harlotries,
    and people with her charms."

X ❧

MAKING USE OF OUR ENGLISH BIBLE

THE OPEN BIBLE

THE Bible is translated into English so that it may be used. The Hebrew Old Testament or the Greek New Testament would be of little use to the average English-speaking person. If Christianity is a religion of the Book, the Book must be available to Christians. And it must be related to more than just the fringes of our lives. It should have a place in private devotions, in public worship, in the life of the family, and in our reading and study.

We cannot tell just how widely used the Bible is. It is easy to say that it is the most sold but least read book in the world. It is probably used more than we are aware. A Gallup poll in 1943 found that sixty-four per cent of the American people read the Bible, but that does not tell us much. It is true that after the Bible has been bought, it often remains unused. The number of volumes of the Scriptures distributed by the American Bible Society in one year has passed considerably the ten million mark. We can say that it is often read not so consistently or so wisely as it might be. Many professing Christians are Biblically illiterate. Some may know the parable of the Prodigal Son or of the Good Samaritan, the story of the Wise Men or of the resurrection of Jesus, but they would have difficulty in recalling the details of the story of Joseph or of the missionary activities of Paul.

The important thing is not merely that the Bible is read. According to Acts 8:30, 31, Philip said to the Ethiopian, " Do you understand what you are reading? " And the Ethiopian replied, " How can I, unless someone guides me? " The Bible should be read with understanding, that the word of God may come to the reader. It is hoped that the comments in this chapter will be of some help to readers of the English Bible.

There is no virtue in reading the Bible without understanding. To do so is as valueless as uttering a prayer when the words come from the lips alone and not from the heart. The words of the Bible are not magical; a reading exercise from the Bible will not act as an incantation to bring good luck to the reader. A soldier is not safer just because he has a copy of the New Testament in his pocket. The Bible is not a fetish or charm. The possession of a copy will not automatically bring good luck to a household.

There is no value in a closed Bible. It is the open Bible, read sincerely and honestly and with a desire to discover the will of God, that has meaning. A family Bible kept in a darkened parlor and used only as a register of births, marriages, and deaths may have a genealogical interest. But the family does not thus automatically grow in the favor of God, nor is It necessarily a Christian home. Men and women who have died as martyrs because they possessed a Bible did not give their lives for the sake of external appearances. They believed in the word in the Bible, not in the binding or the gold-leaf edges.

NEW INTEREST IN THE BIBLE

There does seem to be a revival of interest in the Bible. The number of new translations of the Bible in the twentieth century is some indication of this. The concern of the Division of Christian Education of the National Council of the Churches of Christ in the U.S.A. for a new translation that will find a welcome both in the home and in the churches is not merely an indication that the Bible is not read at present as much as might be hoped. It is itself an indication of increased interest of the churches in the Bible, and of a belief that people want the Bible in living language and will use it. The time seems propitious for such a translation project.

Christian theologians today are becoming more Bible-conscious. A few decades ago there seemed to be a tendency to place an overemphasis on a philosophy of life based largely on the findings of modern science, psychology, and sociology. To some, religion seemed primarily social ethics, and men thought they could lift themselves by their own bootstraps, and a wave of humanism was abroad. Religion should be concerned with social ethics, but we should not forget that Christianity is a historical religion, and its God is the Lord of history, who has revealed himself uniquely in our Jewish-Christian tradition. In some contrast with yesterday, there is today a revival of interest in Biblical theology. Students of the Bible are concerned not merely with the history of the Hebrews and the Early Christian Church, but are asking what the implications of Bible history are for theology.

The Bible is coming to play a larger role in our church school materials, for religious educators are also more Bible-conscious. It is today realized that the entire family must be brought into the picture in connection with the religious education of the children in the church school. The family is asked to co-operate, for Christian education cannot be accomplished adequately in the forty minutes a week allotted to the church school lesson. Through co-operation in such a program the family is coming to appreciate the values in the Bible, not only for the nurture of the children, but for the spiritual welfare of the entire family.

In schools of higher education there seems to be a movement away from the increasing secularization that has existed. Even denominational colleges had often forgotten their religious origins and inspiration, and the Bible had come to have a smaller and smaller place in the college curriculum. Students were graduating from college who were completely Biblically illiterate, and many still are doing so. A teacher of art in a Western college has said that he had to require his students to read the New Testament so that they would be able to appreciate the New Testament themes put on canvas by the great masters. Teachers of English literature often have difficulty because the students are unable to recognize the influence of the Bible on the ideas and language of many of the great authors and poets of the past. The situation seems quite different from the time when the trustees of one Midwestern college voted in 1840 " to expunge from the list of books studied such portions of the heathen classics as pollute and debase the mind, and to restore the Holy Bible to its place as a permanent textbook in the whole course of intellectual training " (R. S. Fletcher, *A History of Oberlin College,* p. 232).

But after World War II, when the colleges and universities made a restudy of their functions and purposes, there was evident a revival of concern for the teaching of religion and the Bible. Religion today is more " respectable " on the campuses of this country, and there are notable experiments in teaching it. Likewise, despite the effect of a recent Supreme Court decision regarding the teaching of religion in the public schools, there is interest in weekday religious education, often on a released-time basis. Most of such teaching is based primarily on Bible study.

How to Read the Bible

The Bible is not an easy book to read. One of the reasons for this is the fact that the Bible is not a single book with a limited message. The Bible is a library of books, sixty-six books in all. It reflects man's search for God and God's revelation of himself to man over a period of many centuries. It arose out of many different kinds of historical and social situations. And it contains many different kinds of literature, such as prose narratives, laws, prophetic oracles or " sermons," hymns, proverbs, and letters. It is the product of many writers. Much of it is not in the proper chronological order of its composition. For example, the Epistles of Paul were written before the Gospels, Mark was written before Matthew, and Amos before Ruth. One who tries to read the Bible from cover to cover may find himself stranded in the long genealogical lists in Genesis or in the complicated laws regarding sacrifice in Leviticus. Some parts of the Bible seem more immediately relevant for our day than other parts.

The situation is not hopeless. If it were, the Bible would never have been read so eagerly and so widely as it has through the centuries. The stories of creation; the careers of Abraham, Joseph, Moses, Samuel, David, and others; the books of Ruth and Jonah; the oracles of the shepherd Amos; the life and teachings of the nearly martyred Jeremiah; the spiritual struggles of Job in the " dark night of the soul "; the dreams of the new age in the books of the prophets; the comforting and inspiring songs of the psalmists; the simple and moving accounts of the Carpenter of Nazareth — these and other things we read in the Scripture and find the word of God to us.

The Bible should be read intelligently. At times one profits from sporadic reading, opening the Bible on special occasions of gladness or sorrow. But the Bible should also be read regularly, if it is to be more fully appreciated and its influence brought to bear more completely on our lives. For this we often need guidance, which may come from the minister, from the church school teacher, or from a good book on the Bible. Myriads of books have been written on how to read the Bible. They tell us what we may expect to find in the Bible, or what passages may most profitably be read, or what order of reading may best be undertaken. A list of more recent good books on this subject would include J. P. Love, *How to Read the Bible* (The Macmillan Company, 1940); E. J. Goodspeed, *How to Read the Bible* (John C. Winston Company, 1946); H. H. Watts, *The Modern Reader's Guide to the Bible* (Harper & Brothers, 1949); D. N. Freedman and J. D. Smart, *God Has Spoken* (The Westminster Press, 1949). To the person who wants to read more understandably such books as the following are also helpful: W. C. Bower, *The Living Bible* (Harper & Brothers, 1936); G. L. Chamberlin, *Making the Bible Live* (University of Chicago Press, 1939); H. L. Willett, *The Bible Through the Centuries* (Willett, Clark & Company, 1929); W. A. Smart, *Still the Bible Speaks* (Abingdon-Cokesbury Press, 1948); E. J. Goodspeed, *Story of the Bible* (University of Chicago Press, 1936). As aids to understanding the archaeology and geography of the Bible we would suggest W. F. Albright, *The Archaeology of Palestine* (Pelican Books, 1951) and G. E. Wright and F. V. Filson, *The Westminster Historical Atlas to the Bible* (The Westminster Press, 1945). There are also a number of so-called " Annotated Bibles," which are Bibles with brief introductions to the various books and with footnote commentaries. One of the best of these is *The Westminster Study Edition of The Holy Bible* (The Westminster Press, 1948).

Encouragement can be given to interest in the Bible through the audio-visual aids that are today available. One may secure moving pictures of Biblical events and personages, and filmstrips and slides on Biblical archaeology, the Bible in art, the stories of the Old and New Testaments, the use of the Bible, and even the making of the English Bible. There are also phonograph records, sometimes to accompany slides, in which the Bible stories are told. Occasional full-length feature movies on Biblical subjects are being made by the great commercial moving picture production houses. Some of these are unusually good, and have brought the Bible stories to thousands who are otherwise Biblically illiterate. Their success is not always due to the glamour with which Hollywood may surround the story, but in large part to the dramatic qualities and human interest of the Biblical story itself. This is not to condone the errors of interpretation which may be in such efforts.

Planned Bible-reading, so that something of the over-all message and meaning of the Bible may become known to us, should be a part of the reading program of the Christian. This requires initiative and a realization of what are the more permanent values in life. Radio and television have resulted in a considerable decrease in general reading by the public. It seems easier to be entertained by the ear and eye just by turning a button. While it does not take more effort to open a book, good reading does take more concentration. In these days of crisis and uncertainty it is important that we learn not to escape the present, but to face it with a knowledge of the foundations of truth and love upon which we must build today if we would have any future for ourselves and our children.

The Bible is often the only history book that people have in the house. It is of course not just a history book, for it is much more than that, and it contains a special kind of history. But by reading it we can discover the hand of God in the long career of man and can gain perspective for living in the present. We can gain appreciation of the things that abide. We are made to feel the importance of the individual in the eternal scheme of things, and in the mind of God, and daily life takes on new significance. We gain poise and purpose through communion with the God of the Scriptures. The gadgets of modern life are seen in more proper relation and we are not distracted by things that are merely temporal, but learn to possess treasures for ourselves that are eternal.

We should at least occasionally read portions of the Bible longer than just a few verses. Many Christians have never had the experience of reading one of the Gospels through in the same manner as one would read a book. Some have been moved by the form and style of the Revised Standard Version of the New Testament to do this for the first time. One can read the Gospel of Mark in about an hour of steady, consistent reading. If a person tries this sometime instead of watching a "Western" on the television, he will find the experience a rewarding one. The entire Book of Amos can be read in about a half hour, and the books of Ruth and Jonah in much less time. Of course one would often want to take longer than this, and pause to consider the significance of what he has read.

One may go to the Bible with no special personal problem in mind, letting the Bible speak to the soul as it will. Or one may seek from the Bible help in times of special crises, searching for inspiration to face difficult days, seeking comfort in time of sorrow, hope in time of despair, calm in the midst of storm, or words to express to God a heart full of gratitude. He who has made himself familiar with the Bible by regular reading will know where to look for passages appropriate to his need.

Many find their religious life deepened and the Word of God coming to their help in times of need because they are able to quote Scripture. There is probably less memorization of Bible verses or passages today than there used to be. There are differences of opinion about its value and the age at which one should begin to memorize. There is no virtue in memorization as such. Reciting the Twenty-third Psalm will not drive away evil spirits or exorcise demons. But life can be enriched by knowing by heart certain great passages from English literature and particularly from the Bible. The Twenty-third Psalm; the One Hundredth Psalm; the familiar words in Micah 6:8 beginning, "He has showed you, O man, what is good"; the Beatitudes; or Paul's great characterization of love in I Cor., ch. 13, are among such passages. When these are learned in youth, their full significance may not be grasped, but this is nevertheless the best although not the only time to learn them. Their rich meaning for us grows as we grow in spirit, and they help us in that growth. Passages to be memorized should be taken from a translation "in the tradition." Included here would be the Revised Standard Version, which retains the familiar rhythm and beauty of such passages.

The Bible and Spiritual Growth

Religious educators today speak a great deal about experience-centered religious education. The ultimate purpose of religious education is spiritual growth, the development of the religious life, the widening of the horizons of faith, the formation of Christian personalities, the development of a sense of responsibility for service in the Kingdom of God. Church school classes should be something more than " Bible classes," if by this is meant only the teaching of knowledge of the content of the Bible. Dean Craig has said that the goal of Christian education is not to teach the Bible, but to generate an inner motivation and an outward expression that is truly Christian. To much the same effect G. E. Wright comments that Scripture has no value except for antiquarian purposes unless it affords the reader a quickening of spirit, a searching of heart, or a cleansing of the soul.

The Bible is something more than a textbook for the history of religions. In itself, memorization of the names of the books of the Bible is of little consequence. There is not much ultimate value in knowing that the Bible in the King James Version contains 3,566,-480 letters and 773,693 words, or that the word " and " occurs 46,227 times. The fact that he knows by heart the story of Joseph or of Paul does not *guarantee* that a person will be a better Christian. The devil himself can quote Scripture, without any appreciative effect on the character of that master of the realm of darkness.

When properly understood and used, the Bible appears as the most important medium for experience-centered religious education — indeed, as the primary source material for experience-centered Christian education. God's revelation of himself as manifested in the Bible was through human experience, the experience of the Hebrew people, of the apostles, and of the Early Christian Church. The gospel story is not an event in a vacuum. Jesus taught not only by the words of the Sermon on the Mount, but by living his message among the people of Palestine. The Gospels are biographies of Jesus and may themselves be called experience-centered. They are not abstract theological teachings. The messages of the prophets cannot be understood apart from the social, political, and religious conditions of their day. The Biblical histories are the story of the experiences of the people of Israel. Biblical religion is " religion in life."

The Bible also has become intricately involved in the experience of men since Biblical days. It can be said to be one of the pillars upon which modern civilization rests. It has, for instance, had an almost incredible influence on literature. Lawrence Nelson has shown something of the extent of its influence on English literature in his book, *Our Roving Bible* (Abingdon-Cokesbury Press, 1945). It has contributed much that is truly democratic in our age. The prophetic emphasis on social ethics, the Biblical view of man created in the image of God, the implications in both the Old Testament and the New Testament for the sanctity of human personality — these things have entered into the warp and woof of our present-day life.

The Bible was the inspiration and guide of the Pilgrim Fathers. It provided inspiration and authority for those who were fighting for the abolition of slavery, such as William Lloyd Garrison, editor of the antislavery *Liberator,* and Harriet Beecher Stowe, author of *Uncle Tom's Cabin.* Lincoln at the age of ten had read the Bible through three times. He often read it in the White House early in the morning while the rest of the household were still asleep. Earlier in the history of this country Thomas Jefferson, Patrick Henry, and John Quincy Adams gave testimony to what it meant to them. Many of our secularly minded people of today do not realize the debt they owe to the Bible, as many of the blessings they now enjoy are due to their ancestors who loved the Scriptures and were moved by them.

THE BIBLE AND THE CHURCH

For most fruitful results the Bible must find use in personal worship, study, and meditation, and in the common religious life of the family. Protestantism with its belief in the priesthood of believers makes the individual rather than the Church the final judge of the significance of the Word of God. But the individual can be this only if there is individual use of the Bible, if individuals come to learn and love the Scriptures. Much depends on the leadership given by the church to its members in this matter. Laymen will be encouraged in personal use of the Bible if they see that the Bible has a central place in the church school and in the pulpit, and if they get guidance from the church leaders.

Sixteen years ago Carl S. Patton wrote that it is time for a renaissance of Biblical preaching. Something of this is taking place. It is in part a result of the new interest in Biblical theology mentioned earlier. It is in part the result of the Bible's having a more important place in the total schedule of courses that the minister has studied while in theological seminary. The trained church leaders should give leadership to the members of the congregation in the use of the Bible. Unlike the Roman Catholic Church, the Protestant Church will do this without dictating to the individual the way in which he must interpret the Bible. Church school teachers' training courses on Biblical subjects make possible more intelligent use of the Bible in church school classes, and this will have some influence on the personal use of the Bible.

The individual Christian and the World Council of Churches may seem at first glance to be far apart from one another. They are in reality very close. The World Council of Churches is an expression of the fact that the Church is a community of believers. The Church is not an organization or a denomination, but the communion of saints, a community of the faithful, a fellowship of people who acknowledge Jesus as the Christ. That fellowship has its origins in the New Testament Church, which was likewise a fellowship, the " one body in Christ " mentioned by Paul in Rom. 12:5. Its roots go back to " the people of the Lord " in the Old Testament. It is in its common faith in the Scriptures that the Christian Church must find one of its bases of unity. Among other ways, the importance of the Bible in the World Council of Churches is indicated by a series of conferences held before the Amsterdam Assembly on the problem of " The Biblical Authority for the Church's Social and Political Message Today." An ecumenical study conference held at Oxford in 1949 issued a document entitled, " Guiding Principles for the Interpretation of the Bible," in which it was agreed that the Christian's authority lies in the will of God, and that the Bible stands in a unique position in mediating that will to us.

We do not think of the Bible in terms of the divisions within Protestantism, for the Bible belongs to the whole community of the faithful. We do not associate the King James Bible with any one Church group. The making of the Revised Standard Version is an interdenominational project, and may be taken in part as a recognition of the place of the Bible in the wider Church fellowship. When we read the Bible, we come to feel that we are a part of that larger community.

THE WORD OF GOD IN LIVING LANGUAGE

The subtitle of this volume implies that the Word of God has meaning for the world in which we live. The Bible should be in living language because it is relevant to life. The Bible should be in language that people can understand because it is to be used by people for understanding the will of God for themselves and for their times. The conviction that this is true has been the great motivating factor in the history of the translation of the Bible.

In tracing a portion of that history we have made a long pilgrimage. It began before the time of Jesus, with the Greek- and Aramaic-speaking Jews seeking translations of the Scripture in the vernacular. In the early Christian centuries came the Syriac and Latin translations. Since our subject has been the English Bible, we have not described the translations of the Bible into other modern languages, for this would require several volumes. In our twelve-hundred-year journey from the time the peasant Caedmon was inspired in a stable to sing the stories of Scripture to the publication of the Revised Standard Version on September 30, 1952, we have met many people and visited many places.

We have met John Wycliffe, William Tyndale, Miles Coverdale, John Rogers, Richard Taverner, William Whittingham, Archbishop Parker, Miles Smith, John Wesley, Noah Webster, R. F. Weymouth, James Moffatt, Edgar Goodspeed, J. M. P. Smith, Luther A. Weigle, and many others involved in the translation of the Bible. Erasmus, Beza, Calvin, Tischendorf, Westcott, Hort, and others have crossed our paths. We have seen Archbishop Thomas Cranmer, Sir Thomas More, Bishop Tunstall, King Henry VIII, King Edward VI, King James I, Queen Mary, and Queen Elizabeth. We have visited Cambridge, Oxford, London, Antwerp, Hamburg, Wittenberg, Worms, Geneva, Zurich, Rheims, Douai, Alexandria, Cairo, Aleppo, Mt. Sinai, Jerusalem, and even Chicago, New Haven, New York, and Cleveland, as well as numerous other places. We have been in church councils, universities, homes, churches, and monasteries. We have witnessed changes in languages and in attitudes toward Bible translations.

But most of all we have watched the efforts to put the Bible into language understood by the people. In so doing we have gained some perspective on the nature of our translated Bible. Some of the problems and techniques of translation may now be better appreciated. The individual who understands something of the history of the English Bible will have a basis of judgment as he considers the values of the numerous translations that one finds today on the shelves of the bookstore. He will possess greater wisdom in his personal selection of the translation which he would use. If he uses more than one translation he should be able to judge their respective values, for different translations may possess diverse values, each often excelling in different qualities. With the complete Revised Standard Version now first appearing on the scene, one should see it not merely from the perspective of the King James Version, but in the light of other translations as well. The Bible reader who knows the history of the English versions will also understand better what is really meant by an " authorized " version, and the differences between translations that are the product of committees and those made by individuals.

He will also be able to read between the lines of the Bible the story of the consecrated lives and scholarly efforts that have gone into the making of the English Bible. He will see there a heroic narrative involving courage, self-sacrifice, devotion, and even martyrdom. There will come before his mind's eye such figures as Wycliffe, Tyndale, Rogers, and Coverdale, upon whose foundations there has been built the Scripture lesson which the student may read so casually in the church school lessons. He will see the emptied grave of Wycliffe, the cold and damp prison cell of Tyndale in the castle of Vilvorde, Rogers' path to the stake, the library of the Monastery of St. Catherine, archaeologists painstakingly removing the debris of the ages from a " mound of many cities," and scholars pouring over manuscripts in the quiet of their studies. He will cherish the

Bible, not alone for its intrinsic worth as it reveals to him the will of God, but also because he knows something of the love and care that have gone into the translation of the Word of God into living language.

APPENDIX

Chapter I

Why should each Christian read the Bible for himself?

What are some of the languages into which the Bible was first translated?

What is the Septuagint? What is the Vulgate?

Who was Jerome? Who was Caedmon? Who was Bede?

Tell as much as you can about the life of John Wycliffe.

Who were the Lollards?

What happened to John Wycliffe's bones?

Did John Wycliffe translate the Bible?

When was the first complete English translation of the Bible made?

Chapter II

Tell as much as you can about William Tyndale's life.

Who was Erasmus? Who was Monmouth? Who was Poyntz?

What effect did the invention of printing have on the circulation of the Bible?

How was Tyndale's translation received?

What did Bishop Tunstall and Sir Thomas More think about Tyndale's New Testament?

Tell about Tyndale's translation work on the Old Testament.

How did Tyndale's translation differ from the Wycliffe Bible?

What influence did Tyndale's translation have on the King James Version?

Chapter III

Tell something about the life and character of Miles Coverdale.

Was Coverdale's Bible a translation from the original Hebrew and Greek?

How did John Rogers contribute to Bible translation?
What was the first "authorized" version of the English Bible?
What was the relation of the Great Bible to Matthew's Bible?
What was the relation of the Bishops' Bible to the Great Bible?
What was Queen Mary's attitude toward Bible translations?
Why was the Genevan Bible translated in Switzerland?
How popular was the Genevan Bible?
What was the Rheims and Douai Version?

Chapter IV

Tell what you can about King James I.
How did the King James Version get started?
How was the King James Version made?
How did some people look upon the King James Version at first?
Discuss the English of the King James Version.
Why has the King James Version been so widely accepted and used?

Chapter V

Why do new translations of the Bible have to be made?
What is the oldest existing manuscript of the complete Old Testament in the original Hebrew?
Tell the story of the discovery of the early manuscript of the Greek Bible in the monastery at Mt. Sinai.
What part did John Wesley and Noah Webster have in Bible translation?
Why was Julia Smith's translation of the Bible not a good translation?
Why was the English Revised Version of 1881–1885 made?
Why was the American Standard Version of 1901 made?
Describe the values and shortcomings of these two versions.
How were they received?

Chapter VI

How can archaeology be of assistance to Bible translation?
Tell about the Canaanite temple library at Ugarit.
Tell the story of the Dead Sea Scrolls.
Why are the Dead Sea Scrolls "the most important manuscript dis-

covery of modern times "?

What is the oldest fragment of manuscript of the New Testament text?

Why is the study of ancient Greek manuscripts of the New Testament important?

What is Koine Greek?

Does such a thing as the " original " manuscript of the Bible exist?

Chapter VII

Why have so many English translations of the Bible been made since 1900?

With what twentieth century translations are you most familiar?

Which one of the " modern " translations do you like best, and why?

Name as many of the twentieth century translations as you can.

What is the importance of Moffatt in Bible translations?

What part has Goodspeed played in modern Bible translations?

Tell something about *The Bible, An American Translation.*

What is the newer attitude of the Catholic Church toward the translation and circulation of the Bible in English?

What are some of the common characteristics of modern English translations of the Bible?

Chapter VIII

Why is the Revised Standard Version needed?

In what respect is it an authorized version?

How was the Revised Standard Version made?

How is it an interdenominational project?

What are the values of a translation of the Bible by a committee?

Tell about the publication of the Revised Standard Version of the New Testament.

Why is the publication of the complete Revised Standard Version an event of importance?

Chapter IX

How has the English language changed since the time when the King James Version was first published?

What is meant by the expression " Bible English "?

What is gained by having the Bible in the English of today?

How does the Revised Standard Version have at the same time both a more consistent translation and a more varied vocabulary?

Read the first chapter of Luke in the King James Version and in the Revised Standard Version, and compare them for literary form, such as paragraphing, punctuation, quotation marks, etc.

Read Isa., ch. 55, in both the King James Version and the Revised Standard Version and see what difference the representation of the poetry in the Revised Standard Version makes.

Look at the footnotes in the Revised Standard Version of The Book of Amos, and discuss their meaning.

Read over together in class the passages quoted in the last part of this chapter, and discuss them.

Chapter X

Does a closed Bible have any value?

What does the expression "the Word of God " mean to you?

Do you know of any evidence of increased interest in the Bible today?

What do you think of planned Bible-reading?

How can the Bible best be used in the home?

What is the value of reading larger sections of the Bible at a time?

How can the Bible provide means of spiritual growth?

How can the use of the Bible in the church be improved?

What are some of the reasons why it is worth-while to know something about the history of the translation of the Bible into English?

INDEX

of Names and Subjects

INDEX OF NAMES AND SUBJECTS